GUIDE TO REUPHOLSTERING

McGraw-Hill Paperbacks
Home Improvement Series

Guide to Plumbing

Guide to Electrical Installation and Repair

Guide to Roof and Gutter Installation and Repair

Guide to Wallpaper and Paint

Guide to Paneling and Wallboard

Guide to Landscape and Lawn Care

Guide to Brick, Concrete, and Stonework

Guide to Carpentry

Guide to Furniture Refinishing and Antiquing

Guide to Bathroom and Kitchen Remodeling

Guide to Reupholstering

Guide to Vegetable Gardening and Preserving

Guide to Bicycle Repair and Maintenance

Guide to Floor and Carpeting Installation and Repair

GUIDE TO REUPHOLSTERING

McGraw-Hill Book Company

New York   St. Louis   San Francisco   Auckland   Bogotá   Guatemala   Hamburg
Johannesburg   Lisbon   London   Madrid   Mexico   Montreal   New Delhi
Panama   Paris   San Juan   São Paulo   Singapore   Sydney   Tokyo   Toronto

1 2 3 4 5 6 7 8 9 0 SMSM 8 6 5 4 3 2 1

Library of Congress Cataloging in Publication Data

Main entry under title:

Guide to reupholstering.

(McGraw-Hill paperbacks home improvement series)
Originally issued in 1975 by the Automotive-Hardware Trades
Division of the Minnesota Mining and Manufacturing Company
under title: The home pro reupholstering guide.
1. Upholstery. I. Minnesota Mining and Manufacturing
Company. Automotive-Hardware Trades Division. Home pro
reupholstering guide.
TT198.G84   684.1'2   80-18021
ISBN 0-07-045971-1 (pbk.)

Cover photo courtesy of World Carpets, Dalton, Georgia

Contents ▬▬▬▬▬▬▬▬▬▬

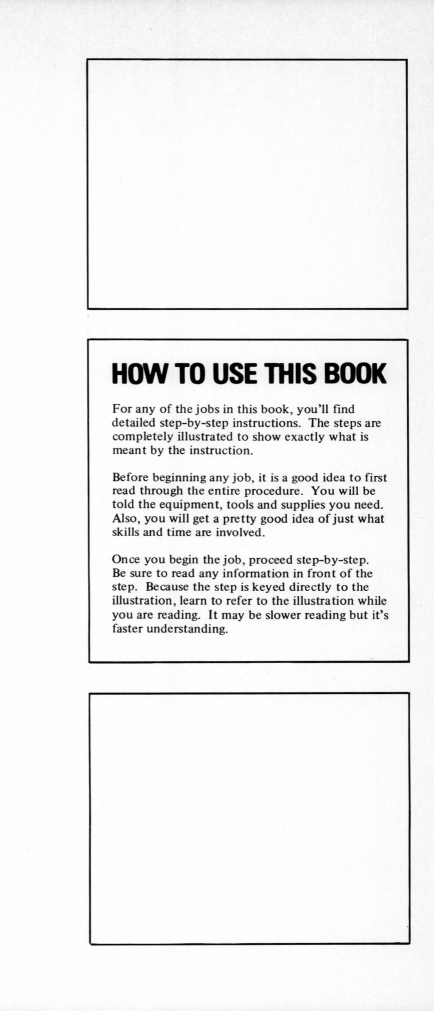

HOW TO USE THIS BOOK

For any of the jobs in this book, you'll find detailed step-by-step instructions. The steps are completely illustrated to show exactly what is meant by the instruction.

Before beginning any job, it is a good idea to first read through the entire procedure. You will be told the equipment, tools and supplies you need. Also, you will get a pretty good idea of just what skills and time are involved.

Once you begin the job, proceed step-by-step. Be sure to read any information in front of the step. Because the step is keyed directly to the illustration, learn to refer to the illustration while you are reading. It may be slower reading but it's faster understanding.

GUIDE TO REUPHOLSTERING

REUPHOLSTERY

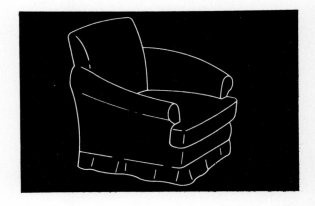

There are many types and styles of upholstered furniture. They can be greatly different from each other in appearance. Even one style of furniture, for example, wing back chairs, can present a wide variety of appearances.

However, all upholstered furniture has more in common than appearances would indicate. They all have the same basic function, seating comfort, and are very much alike in their basic construction.

The purpose of this section is to show how a typical piece of upholstered furniture is constructed. It also shows the variations that you may find in the basic construction. For example, cushioning may be accomplished with springs or foam padding. If springs are used, they may be coil springs or S-shaped springs called sagless springs. You will learn about them here.

Most of the illustrations in the book are based on wing back chairs. It is among the more challenging styles of furniture to reupholster. Also, it represents most of the variations in construction that you are likely to find in your particular project.

Read this section carefully so that you will know what to expect when you begin your reupholstery project.

The main sections of a wing back chair are:

Wings [1]
Back [2]
Arms [3]
Seat [4]
Show wood [5]. Any wood that is exposed, such as legs or decorative panels on arms or backs, is called show wood. Some chairs may have no show wood at all. Other chairs may consist almost entirely of show wood. Only the seat and back panel may be upholstered.

If show wood must be repaired or refinished, this work should be done right after you install the muslin cover on the furniture and before you install the new top cover.

The seat [4] consists of the following parts:

Outside cover [6]
Padding [7]
Burlap cover [8]
Springs [9]. Coil springs as illustrated are most commonly used in seats. However, sagless springs are sometimes used.
Frame [10]

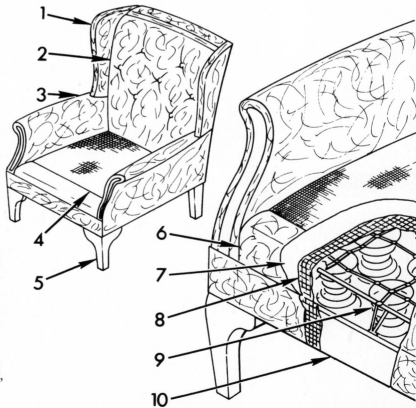

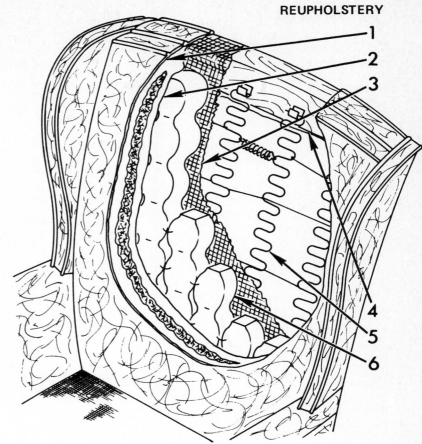

The back of a chair consists of the following parts:

    Top cover [1]
    Padding [2]
    Burlap cover [3]
    Frame [4]
    Springs [5, 6] or other cushioning. On some
        chairs sagless springs [5] are used to pro-
        vide support for cushioning made up of
        many lightweight coil springs [6]. The
        entire assembly of coil springs is called
        a Marshall unit.

In many chairs, the back cushion will be
made of polyurethane foam instead of
springs. If furniture has springs which
are damaged, it is recommended that
they be removed and replaced with polyurethane foam. The foam is easy to cut
and shape and it has excellent cushioning
qualities.

Upholstered arms consist of the following parts:

    Top cover [1]
    Padding [2]
    Frame [3]

In some cases, webbing will also be found in
arms. The purpose of the webbing is to
support the padding which is used to shape
the arm.

The wings on a chair are strictly decorative.
They are made in many different shapes and
sizes. Some wings are so small that they are
scarcely noticed. Other wings are very large
and deep. Wings consist of the following
parts:

    Top cover [4]
    Padding [5]
    Frame [6]

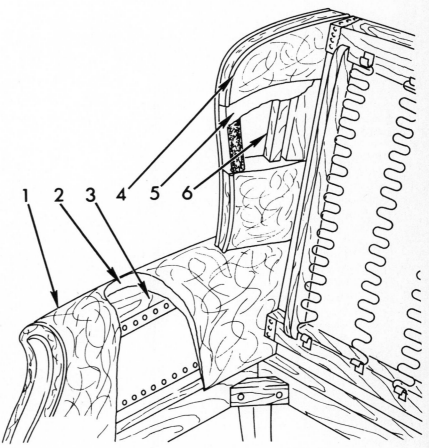

REUPHOLSTERY

The basic support for the chair is the frame. The furniture can only be as good as the frame. If the frame is broken or is constructed of poor quality wood, it is usually recommended that the furniture not be reupholstered. The furniture may not be worth the investment in time and materials.

The frame consists of most or all of the following parts:

Top wing rails [1]
Wing slats [2]
Wing posts [3]
Top rail [4]
Back slats [5]
Side posts [6]
Front seat rail [7]
Back seat rails [8]
Back liner [9]
Side seat rails [10]
Arm stumps [11]
Arm boards [12]
Arm liners [13]
Arm slats [14]

These parts will be referred to many times in the reupholstery procedures. In many cases, they provide the support to which all other parts are fastened. Study their names and locations.

While the frame provides the form and support for the furniture, the comfort of the item depends largely upon the cushioning.

Cushioning is commonly provided by springs or polyurethane foam. If springs are used, one or both of the following kinds may be used in a single item:

Sagless springs [1]
Coil springs [4]

Sagless springs [1] are often used in the backs of furniture. However, in many kinds of items, such as office chairs, sagless springs are also used in seats.

If sagless springs are used in backs, they are frequently covered with a Marshall unit [2]. A Marshall unit is composed of many lightweight coil springs, enclosed in individual pockets. They form a soft cushion.

Sagless springs are fastened to the frame with clips. They are covered with burlap [3] to provide a support for padding material.

Sagless springs are very durable and seldom need repair.

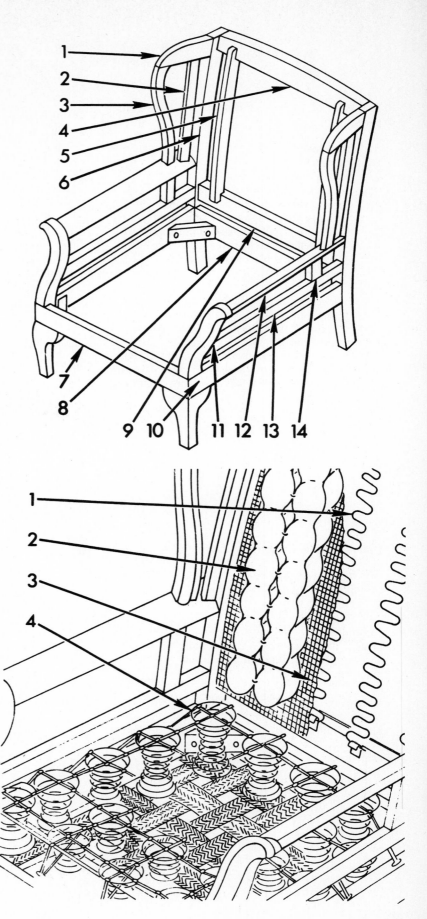

4

Coil springs [1] are commonly used in seats. They are often used in removable cushions as well as in the seat which supports the removable cushion. The coil springs are supported in the frame with webbing [2].

Webbing used in upholstery is made of 3-1/2 inch wide strips of jute. The strips of webbing are held to the frame with tacks. The coil springs are fastened to the webbing with stitches or clips.

The springs are tied at their correct height and position with twine. They are covered with burlap [3] to prevent padding material from being forced into the springs. Sometimes the padding and burlap will be held in place over the springs by stitching them directly to the springs.

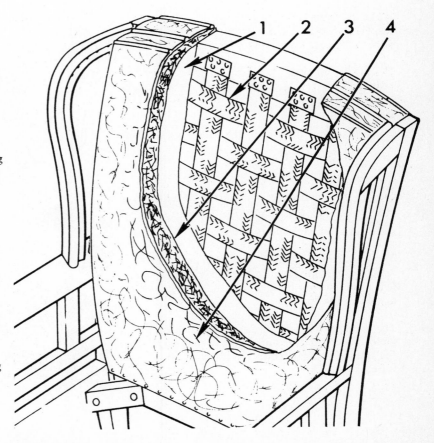

Many times polyurethane foam [1] will be used for cushioning rather than springs. The foam is supported by webbing [2]. It is covered with padding [3] and the top cover [4].

Padding is used for several purposes:

- It gives the furniture its final shape. Padding is made of cotton batting, moss, hair or thin layers of polyurethane foam. Cotton is almost always found. The other materials may or may not be present.

  Cotton is always the top layer of padding. It is extremely easy to shape and provides a smooth, even surface to upholster.

- Padding is used to soften surfaces and corners of the frame. It therefore prolongs the life of the top cover by eliminating hard wear spots.

- Padding increases the comfort or cushioning effect of the furniture.

REUPHOLSTERY

The last part to be installed on the furniture is the top cover. Many materials are available for covering upholstered furniture. Special upholstery fabrics, leather and soft, pliable plastics are used.

The top cover is made up of several smaller sections. The top cover sections are fastened to the frame with tacks and to each other with hand or machine sewn seams. The cover sections for a wing back chair are:

Wings [1]
Back [2]
Arms [3]
Seat [4]

The seat cover may be a one piece cover, or a cover with one or more of the following sections:

Box strips [5]
Band strip [6]
Skirt [7]

The box strip is a strip of top cover material which is machine sewn to the seat cover. It is installed over the padding and springs and tacked to the frame.

The band strip is a strip of top cover material which covers the front and possibly side parts of the frame. It is tacked to the frame at all four sides.

The skirt is a strip of top cover material which covers the front and possibly side parts of the frame and legs. It is usually pleated and is free on the bottom edge.

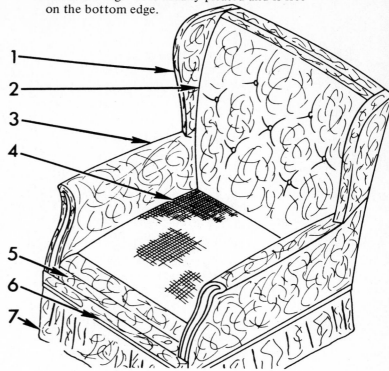

The back cover consists of at least two sections:

Inside back cover [1]
Outside back cover [2]

It may have one or both of the following sections:

Box strip [3]
Band strip [4]

The inside back cover covers the padding. The outside back cover covers the internal parts as seen from the backside of the chair.

The box strip is a strip of top cover material which is machine sewn to the inside back cover. It is installed over the padding and springs and tacked to the frame.

The band strip is a strip of top cover material which covers the top and possibly side parts of the frame. It is tacked to the frame at all four sides.

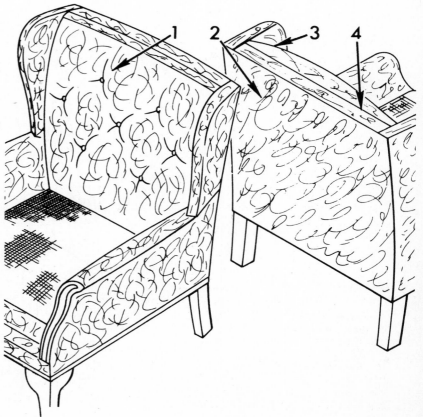

6

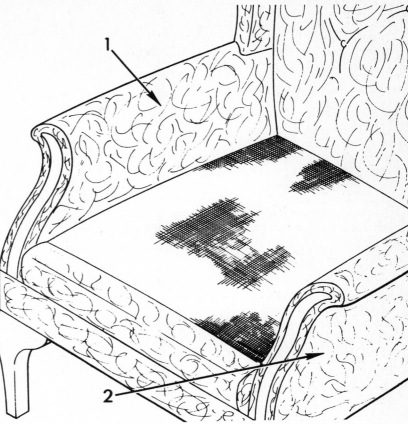

The arm cover usually consists of two sections:

    Inside arm [1]
    Outside arm [2]

The inside arm cover covers the padding. The outside arm cover covers the internal parts as seen from the outside of the arm.

In some cases, the outside arm cover may consist of a panel which is covered with the top cover material and tacked or glued to the frame.

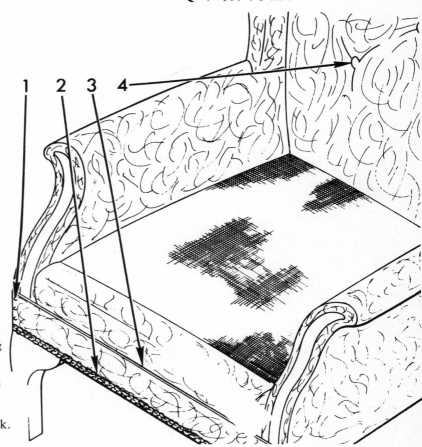

A number of decorative items are used in furniture construction. They may be found on any of the top cover sections. Decorative items are:

    Decorative tacks [1]
    Gimp [2]
    Welting [3]
    Buttons [4]

Decorative tacks are tacks with heads which are designed to add to the beauty of the furniture. They are used to secure the top cover to the frame.

Gimp is a braided or decorative strip of material used to cover tacks or staples that hold the top cover to the frame. It is fastened to the cover with glue.

Welting is a strip of cord covered with the top cover material. In some cases, a contrasting material is used. The welting is used between individual sections of a top cover. It is fastened by machine sewing it to the top cover or tacking it to the frame.

Buttons are used to create a decorative effect on furniture. They are often used on backs to provide interest. Sometimes they are also found on seats. Buttons are required to make a tufted back.

REUPHOLSTERY

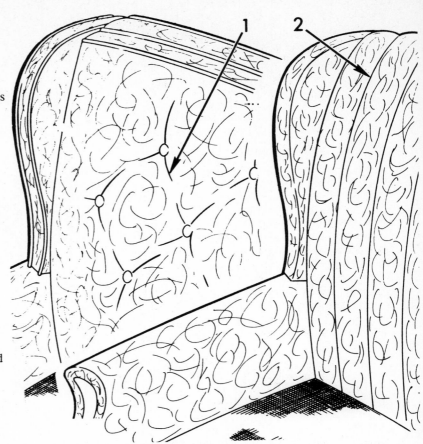

Special decorative treatments which are sometimes found in upholstered furniture are:

    Tufting [1]
    Channeling [2]

Tufting usually has the appearance of large, diamond-shaped or square-shaped patterns. The patterns are made up of buttons which are deeply embedded in the surface of the inside back cover. They are connected together by deep creases in the top cover to form the pattern. Tufts are sometimes found in arms and seats as well as backs.

Channeling has the appearance of long ridges separated by deep creases. They are made by sewing and stuffing the top cover before installing on the furniture. Channels are usually found only on backs. However, they are sometimes used on arms and seats too.

■■ TOOLS AND SUPPLIES ■■

▶ Tools

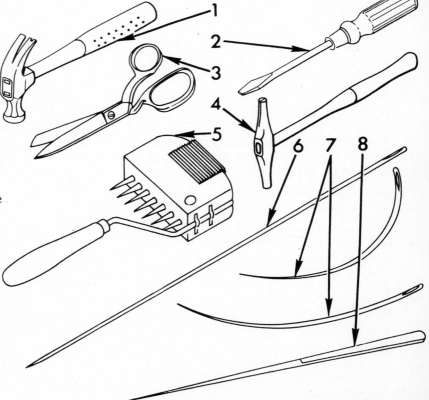

A number of common tools and some special purpose tools are required to do a professional looking job. These special tools are relatively inexpensive and should be obtained to ensure good results.

    Hammer [1] or mallet
    Common screwdriver [2] or ripping tool for
        removing tacks from frame
    Scissors [3] or shears
    Magnetic tack hammer [4]
    Webbing stretcher [5] for installing new jute
        webbing bands
    12-inch straight upholstery needle [6] for
        installing buttons
    3-inch and 5-inch curved upholstery
        needle [7] for blind-stitching
    Cloth measuring tape
    Iron
    Stuffing regulator [8] for arranging padding
        after the muslin cover is installed

Tools

Sewing machine with zipper foot or commercial upholstery sewing machine. Commercial upholstery sewing machine can be rented from an upholstery dealer or tool rental agency.

Electric knife for cutting polyurethane foam

Two yardsticks or two thin flat boards for stuffing padding into a channeled back

▶ **Supplies**

3 oz (No. 3) tacks for installing muslin cover

4 oz (No. 4) tacks for installing burlap cover or new top cover

12 oz (No. 12) tacks or 14 oz (No. 14) tacks for installing webbing bands or spring twine

Upholsterer's cotton padding for replacing worn cotton padding

Burlap for covering springs or polyurethane foam padding

Muslin for covering padding before installing top cover

Spring twine for tying coil springs

5/22-inch welt cord for making welting strips

Cardboard strips for blind tacking top cover to frame

Carpet thread for blind stitching top cover sections together

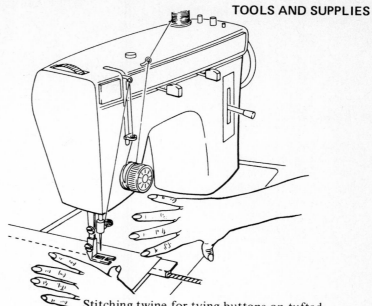

Stitching twine for tying buttons on tufted backs

Reupholstering will be much easier if you work at a comfortable work height. A good work platform can be constructed by covering a table or bench with a blanket. Tie the blanket securely to keep it from sliding around. Place the piece being reupholstered on the platform as required to obtain convenient access to parts.

DISASSEMBLY AND INSPECTION

Before beginning to reupholster a chair be sure to read Pages 2 through 8 to familiarize yourself with the construction of a chair.

If your chair has a tufted or channeled inside back cover, be sure to read Pages 78 through 81 for installing a tufted back or Pages 81 through 83 for installing a channeled back.

Before removing any section of the top cover, carefully examine it to determine how and where it is attached to the frame.

The following information must be observed and recorded for each section of top cover to aid in installing the new top cover:

● The frame rails to which the section is attached.

● For each frame rail, the particular side of the rail used for attaching the section.

● The type and approximate number of tacks holding the section to a rail.

● The distance between tacks.

● The location of blind stitches joining one section to another.

When installing the new top cover, these notes must be used as an aid to insure the cover is installed correctly.

After each section is removed, use chalk to label the section.

When reupholstering a chair be sure to follow this sequence:

● Inspect chair

● Remove cambrick dust cover

● Remove skirt, if installed

● Remove outside back cover

● Remove outside arm cover

● Remove inside back cover

● Remove outside wing cover, if installed

● Remove inside wing cover, if installed, and make necessary repairs

● Inspect back and make any necessary repairs

● Install muslin cover on inside back

● Remove inside arm cover

● Inspect arm and make necessary repairs

● Install muslin cover on inside arm

● Remove seat cover

● Inspect seat and make necessary repairs

● Install muslin cover on seat

● Install top cover

▶ **Inspection**

Before beginning to reupholster the chair, you should inspect it thoroughly to determine what repairs are needed. Inspect the outside before beginning any dismantling.

First, the chair frame should be firm and strong. Check that the chair does not rock from front to back or side to side and that the arms and back are securely attached to the seat.

If the frame is not firm and strong, the chair must be completely disassembled and the frame repaired. Because of the difficulty of total disassembly and assembly, it is recommended that you do not attempt to reupholster a chair with an unsound frame.

Inspection

The back or seat will most commonly be supported in one of the following ways:

- Webbing bands and polyurethane foam [1]
- Webbing bands and coil springs [2]
- Sagless springs [3]

A sagging back or seat usually indicates that the support is defective. If back or seat is sagging, the chair will have to be disassembled until the support can be inspected and repaired.

Hard lumps that cannot be easily depressed also usually indicate that the support is defective. If back or seat has hard lumps, the chair will have to be disassembled until the support can be inspected and repaired.

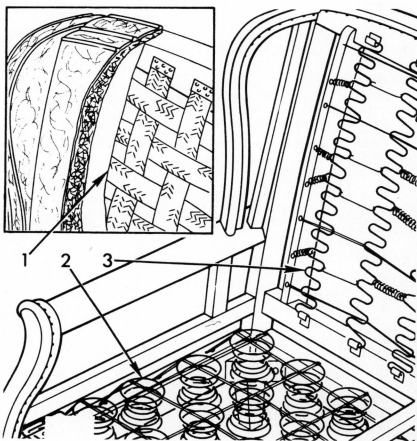

1 2 3

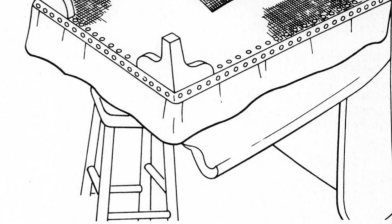

▶ Removing Cambrick Dust Cover

The cambrick dust cover [3] is a panel of stiff, coarse, black material. It is fastened to the bottom of the seat with tacks. It must be removed to allow access to the tacks holding the top cover sections to the frame.

A tack is removed by forcing the blade of a common screwdriver or ripping tool under the tack head and prying the tack from the wood.

When removing a tack, always force the tack in the same direction as the wood grain [1]. By forcing the tack across the wood grain, you could split the wood.

1. Using hammer and screwdriver, remove all tacks [2] holding cambrick dust cover [3] to frame. Remove cambrick dust cover.

▶ Removing Top Cover from Bottom Seat Rails

The different sections of the top cover are attached to the bottom of the seat rails with tacks.

The sections are installed in layers of material over the bottom rails. Each layer is tacked over the preceding layer.

After all tacks holding one layer to the rails are removed, the layer can be pulled away from the rail to expose the tacks holding the next layer to the frame.

If the seat has webbing bands, the tacks holding the bands to the rail will be exposed after all the layers of the top cover material are free. DO NOT remove the tacks holding the webbing bands to the rail.

Be sure to force the tacks in the direction of the wood grain.

1. Using hammer and screwdriver, remove all tacks [1] holding all layers of top cover material to the bottom seat rails.

DISASSEMBLY AND INSPECTION

► **Removing Skirt**

If the chair has a skirt [3], the skirt must be removed before the top cover sections can be removed from the chair.

If the chair does not have a skirt, go to section below.

The skirt is blind tacked to the frame at the top edge of the skirt.

Before removing the skirt, observe and record necessary information. Page 9.

Be sure to force the tacks in the direction of the wood grain.

1. Using hammer and screwdriver, remove all tacks [2] holding skirt [3] to frame. Remove cardboard strip [1]. Remove skirt [3].

2. Using chalk, label skirt [3].

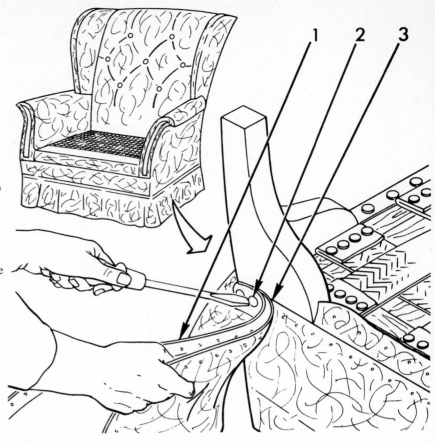

► **Removing Outside Back Cover**

The outside back cover is usually attached to the frame by one or more of the following methods:

- Decorative tacks at top and sides [1]
- Tacks or staples covered with gimp at top and sides [2]
- Blind stitches at sides [3]
- Blind tacks at top [4]

Before removing the outside back cover, observe and record the necessary information. Page 9.

When removing decorative tacks, the head of the tack may break from the shaft. If the head breaks from the shaft, either remove the shaft from the frame with pliers or drive the shaft into the frame with a hammer.

Be sure to force the tacks in the direction of the wood grain.

1. Using hammer and screwdriver, remove all decorative tacks holding cover to frame. Remove cover, if possible.

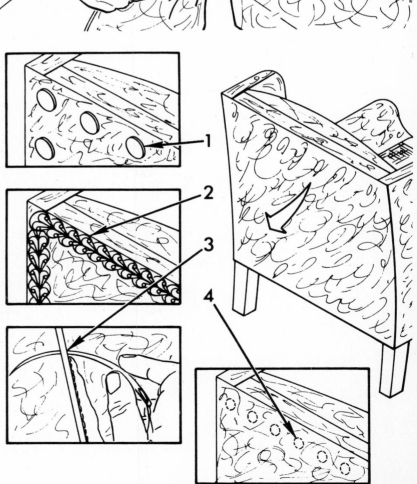

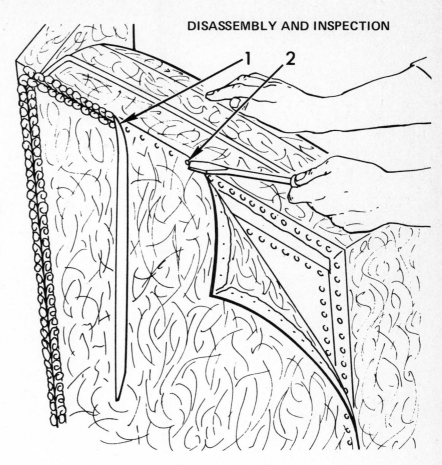

Removing Outside Back Cover

If the cover is attached by tacks [2] or staples covered by gimp [1], the gimp must be removed before the tacks or staples can be removed. Gimp is held to the cover with glue.

Before removing the gimp, observe and record the location of the gimp.

2. Pull all gimp [1] from cover.

3. Remove all tacks [2] or staples holding cover to frame. Remove cover, if possible.

Removing Outside Back Cover

Blind stitches are hand-sewn stitches. They may be used to attach the outside back cover to the inside back cover and outside arm cover.

Blind stitches can be reached by pulling the outside back cover away from the frame exposing the stitches down the side of the cover.

4. Cut and remove all blind stitches [1] holding outside back cover to inside back cover and outside arm cover.

5. Remove all tacks [3] holding cover to frame. Remove cardboard strip [2]. Remove cover.

6. Using chalk, label outside back cover.

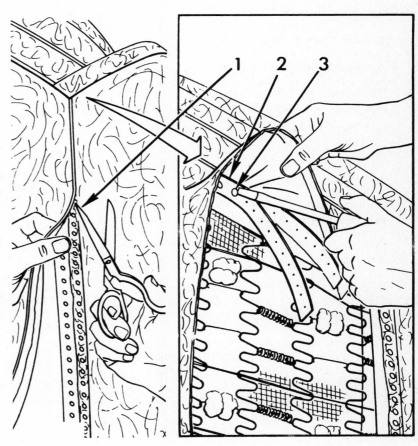

13

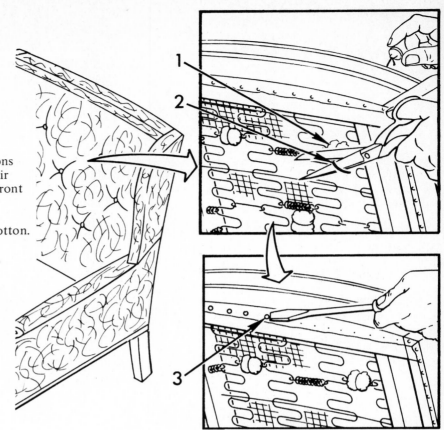

Removing Outside Back Cover

If the inside back cover has buttons, the buttons will be tied to pieces of cotton [1] on the chair back. The twine [2] must be cut before the front cover can be removed.

6. Cut twine [2] at cotton [1]. Remove cotton.

If the back has a burlap or cardboard backing, it must be removed.

7. Remove all tacks [4] holding backing to frame. Remove backing.

▶ Removing Outside Arm Cover

The outside arm cover is usually attached to the frame by one or more of the following methods:

- Decorative tacks at top and sides [1]
- Tacks or staples covered with gimp at top and sides [2]
- Blind stitches at front [3]
- Tacks at front and back [4]
- Blind tacks at top [5]

Before removing the outside arm cover, observe and record necessary information. Page 9.

If the head of a decorative tack breaks from the shaft, remove the shaft with pliers or drive the shaft into frame with a hammer.

1. Remove all decorative tacks holding cover to frame. Remove cover if possible.

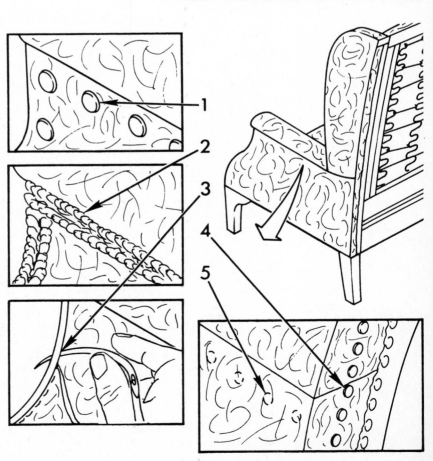

Removing Outside Arm Cover

If the cover is attached by tacks [1] or staples covered with gimp [3], the gimp must be removed before the tacks or staples can be removed.

Before removing the gimp, observe and record the location of the gimp.

2. Pull all gimp [3] from cover [2].

3. Remove all tacks [1] or staples holding cover to frame. Remove cover, if possible.

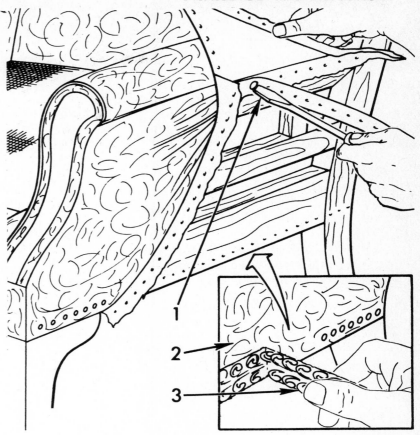

Removing Outside Arm Cover

Some chairs may have a show wood panel or a panel covered with top cover material attached to the front edge of the chair.

This panel [1] must be removed before the outside arm cover can be removed.

If the panel is made of show wood, be careful not to damage the wood when removing the panel.

When removing the panel, note and record how the panel is attached to the frame.

4. Using screwdriver, carefully pry panel [1] from frame.

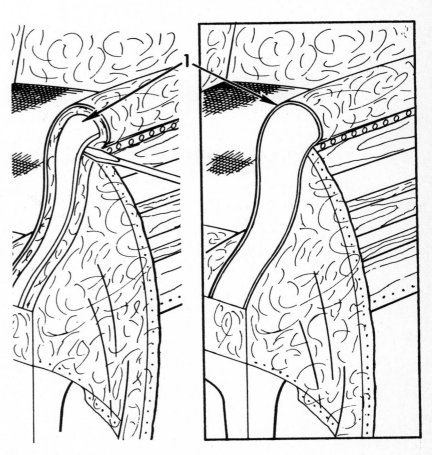

Removing Outside Arm Cover

Blind stitches are loose, hand-sewn stitches. They may be used to attach the outside arm cover to the inside arm cover.

Blind stitches can be reached by pulling the outside arm cover away from the frame exposing the stitches down the side of the cover.

5.   Cut and remove all blind stitches [1 or 2] holding outside arm cover to inside arm cover.

The cover may be attached at the back with tacks. If the arm has a show wood panel, the cover may also be tacked at the front.

Be sure to force tacks in the direction of the wood grain.

6.   Remove all tacks holding cover to front and back of frame.

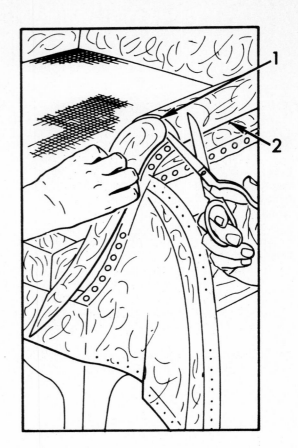

Removing Outside Arm Cover

7.   Remove all blind tacks [1] holding cover to frame. Remove cardboard strip [2]. Remove cover.

8.   Using chalk, label outside arm cover.

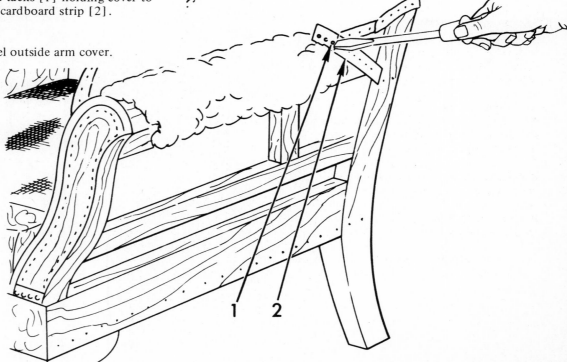

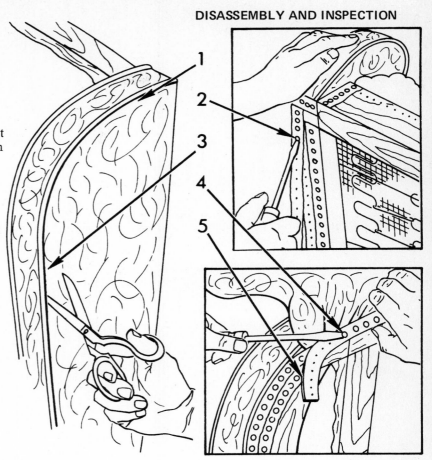

▶ Removing Outside Wing Cover

The outside wing cover is attached to the frame at the bottom and back with tacks, at the front with blind stitches, and at the top with blind tacks.

Before removing outside wing cover, observe and record necessary information. Page 9.

1. Remove all tacks [2] holding back edge and bottom edge of cover [1] to frame.

2. Cut and remove all blind stitches [3].

3. Remove all blind tacks [4] holding cover [1] to frame. Remove cardboard [5]. Remove cover.

4. Using chalk, label outside wing cover.

▶ Removing Inside Back Cover

If the inside back cover has a band strip [1], the strip must be removed before the cover can be removed.

A welting strip [2] may be sewn to the band strip or tacked to the frame. If welting strip is not sewn to the band strip, the welting strip must be removed before the band strip can be removed.

If welting strip is sewn to the band strip, the welting strip and band strip are removed together.

Before removing inside back cover, observe and record necessary information. Page 9.

1. Remove all tacks holding welting strip [2] to frame. Remove welting strip.

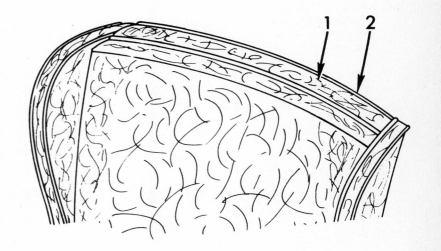

DISASSEMBLY AND INSPECTION

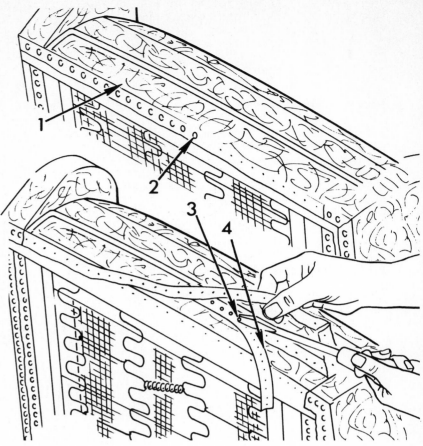

Removing Inside Back Cover

The band strip [1] is attached to the frame with tacks [2] at the back edge and blind tacks [3] at the front edge.

2. Remove all tacks [2] holding back edge of band strip to frame.

3. Remove all blind tacks [3] holding front edge of band strip to frame. Remove cardboard [4]. Remove band strip [1].

4. Using chalk, label band strip.

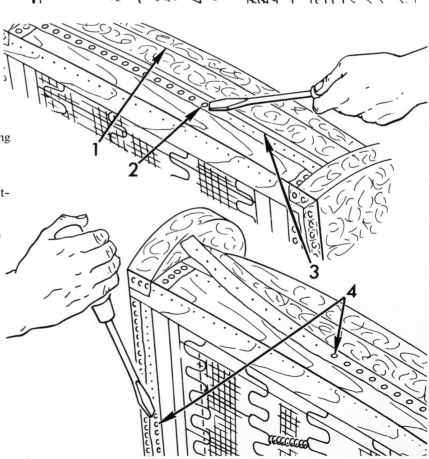

Removing Inside Back Cover

A welting strip [3] may be sewn to the inside back cover [1] or tacked to the frame. If the welting strip is not sewn to the cover, the welting strip must be removed before the cover can be removed.

If the welting strip is sewn to the cover, the welting strip and cover are removed together.

5. Remove all tacks [2] holding welting strip to frame. Remove welting strip [3].

6. Remove all tacks [4] holding inside back cover [1] to frame.

When removing the cover, be careful not to rearrange or move the padding.

7. Carefully remove inside back cover [1].

8. Using chalk, label inside back cover.

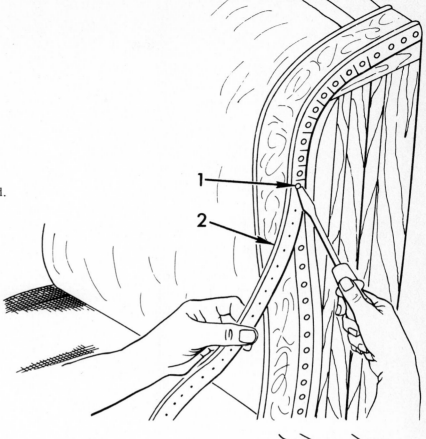

► **Removing Inside Wing Cover**

The inside wing cover is attached to the frame on all four sides with tacks.

A welting strip [2] may be sewn to the inside wing cover or tacked to the frame. If the welting strip is not sewn to the cover, the welting strip must be removed before the cover can be removed.

If the welting strip is sewn to the cover, the welting strip and cover are removed together.

Before removing inside wing cover, observe and record necessary information. Page 9.

1.   Remove all tacks [1] holding welting strip [2] to frame. Remove welting strip.

Removing Inside Wing Cover

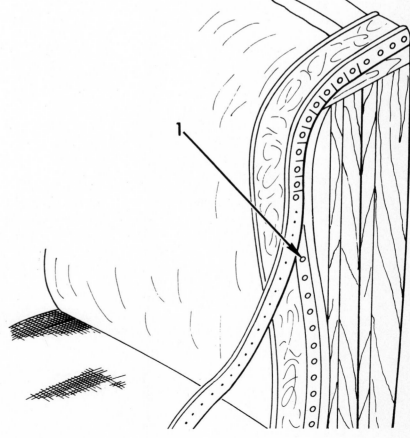

2.   Remove all tacks [1] holding inside wing cover to frame.

When removing the cover, do not move or rearrange padding.

3.   Carefully remove inside wing cover.

4.   Using chalk, label inside wing cover.

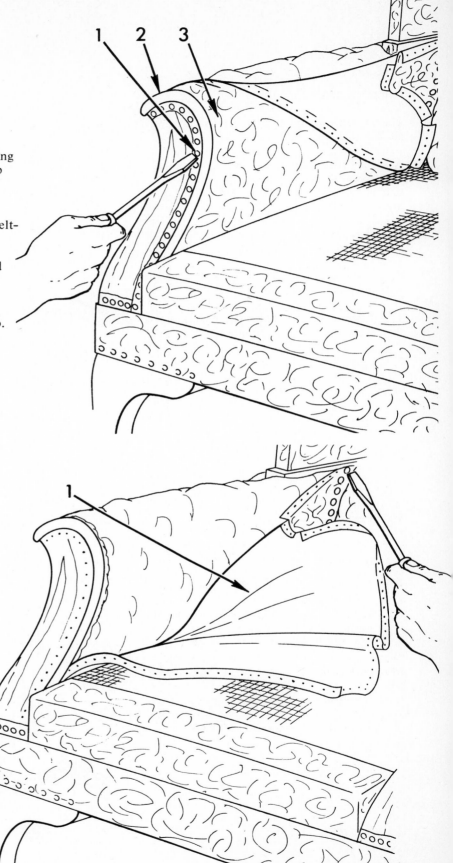

▶ Removing Inside Arm Cover

A welting strip [2] may be sewn to the inside arm cover or tacked to the frame. If the welting strip is not sewn to the cover, the welting strip must be removed before the cover can be removed.

If the welting strip is sewn to the cover, the welting strip and cover are removed together.

Before removing inside arm cover, observe and record necessary information. Page 9.

1. Remove all tacks [1] holding welting strip [2] to frame. Remove welting strip.

Removing Inside Arm Cover

2. Remove all tacks holding inside arm cover [1] to frame.

When removing the cover, be careful not to move or rearrange the padding.

3. Carefully remove inside arm cover [1].

4. Using chalk, label inside arm cover.

► **Removing Seat Cover**

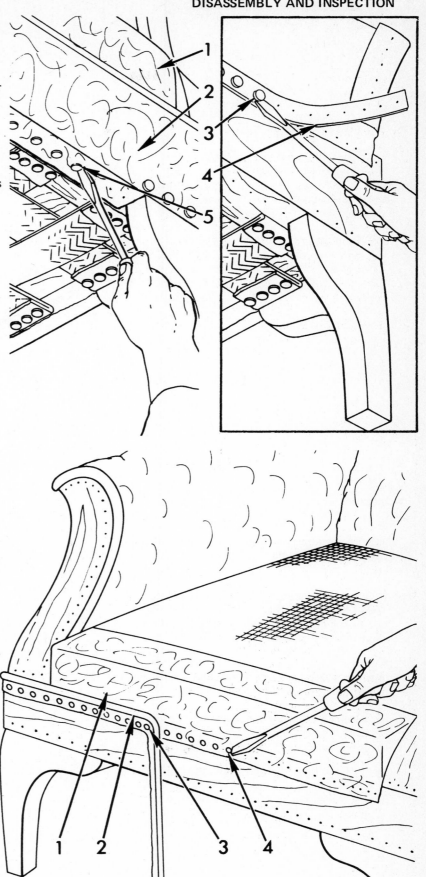

If the seat cover does not have a band strip [2] or a box strip [1], the cover will be free at all edges. The cover can be removed. Go to Page 22.

If the seat cover has a band strip [2] it must be removed before the seat cover can be removed.

The band strip is attached to the frame with tacks on the bottom edge and blind tacks on the top edge.

Before removing seat cover, observe and record necessary information. Page 9.

1. Remove all tacks [5] holding bottom edge of band strip [2] to frame.

2. Remove all blind tacks [3] holding top edge of band strip [2] to frame. Remove cardboard [4]. Remove strip [2].

3. Using chalk, label band strip.

Removing Seat Cover

If the seat cover has a box strip [1], the box strip and seat cover are removed together.

The box strip is attached to the frame with tacks on the bottom front edge.

A welting strip [2] may be sewn to the box strip [1] or tacked to the frame. If the welting strip is not sewn to the box strip, the welting strip must be removed before the cover can be removed.

4. Remove all tacks [3] holding welting strip [2] to frame. Remove welting strip.

5. Remove all tacks [4] holding bottom front edge of box strip [1] to frame.

21

DISASSEMBLY AND INSPECTION

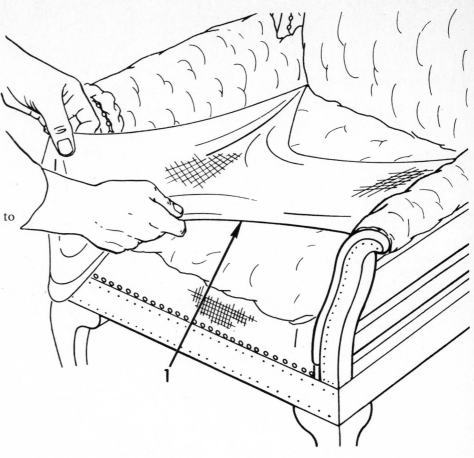

Removing Seat Cover

When removing the cover, be careful not to
rearrange or move the padding.

6.   Remove inside seat cover [1].

7.   Using chalk, label seat cover.

▶ **Inspecting Back and Seat**

If you determined from the inspection that the
back or seat does not need repairing, the muslin
cover must be installed. Go to Page 46 to install
muslin cover.

If you determined from the inspection that
repairs are needed, the back or seat must be disassembled and visually inspected to determine
what repairs are needed.

When removing internal parts, remove them only
until the defective part is identified. Then begin
reassembling the back or seat.

An edge roll [1] may be located on the wooden
edges of the back and seat or on spring edges of
the seat.

1.   Check that edge roll [1] is firm and even.

If edge roll is not firm and even, it must be
replaced. Go to Pages 43 or 44 to replace
edge roll.

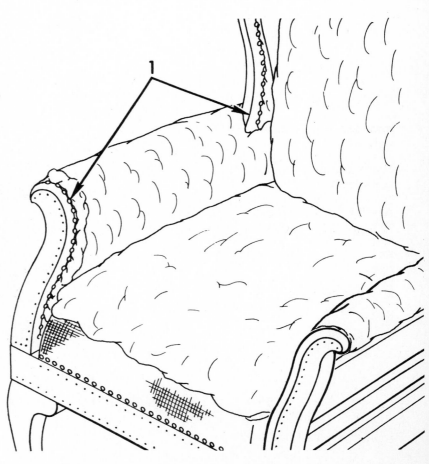

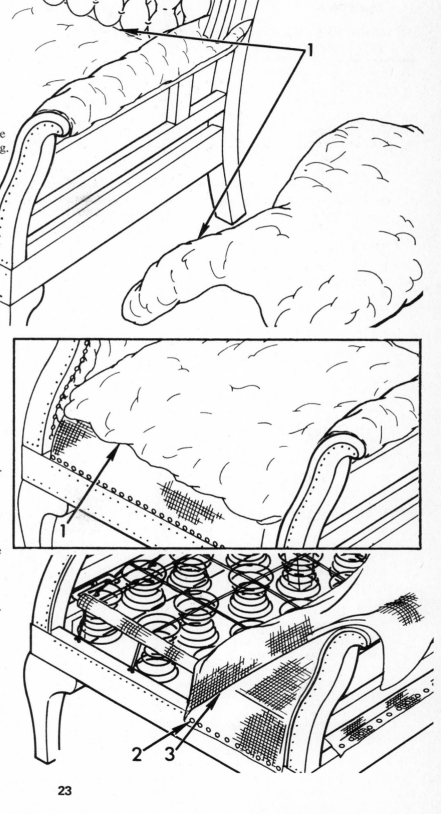

Inspecting Back and Seat

2.   Check that cotton padding [1] is not worn
      or deteriorating.

If the padding is worn or deteriorating, it must be
replaced. Go to Page 46 to install cotton padding.

Inspecting Back and Seat

The next section of padding will consist of one or
more layers of moss or hair padding.

3.   Check that layers of moss or hair
      padding [1] are not worn or deteriorating.

If the padding is worn or deteriorating, it must be
replaced. Go to Page 43 to install padding.

The burlap cover must be removed before the
back supports and seat supports can be inspected.

4.   Remove all tacks [2] holding burlap
      cover [3] to frame. Remove cover.

DISASSEMBLY AND INSPECTION

▶ **Inspecting Back and Seat Support**

After the burlap cover is removed, the back and seat supports can be inspected.

If the support is sagless springs, go to Page 25.

If the support is coil springs and webbing bands, go to Page 24.

If the support is polyurethane foam and webbing bands, continue.

▶ **Inspecting Polyurethane Foam Support**

1. Check that polyurethane foam [2] is not worn or deteriorating.

2. Check that webbing bands [1] are not worn, torn or deteriorating.

If only polyurethane foam is defective, it must be replaced. Go to Page 43 to replace polyurethane foam.

If only webbing bands are defective, they must be replaced. Go to Page 28 to replace webbing bands.

If both polyurethane foam and webbing bands are defective, the webbing bands must be replaced before the foam is replaced. Go to Page 28 to replace webbing bands.

▶ **Inspecting Coil Spring Support**

1. Check that webbing bands [1] are not worn, torn or deteriorating.

2. Check that coil springs [2] are not bent or broken.

3. Check that coil springs [2] compress and return to their correct height.

If only coil springs are defective, they must be replaced. Go to Page 33 to replace springs.

If only webbing bands are defective, they must be replaced. Go to Page 28 to replace webbing bands.

If both coil springs and webbing bands are defective, the webbing bands must be replaced before the springs are replaced. Go to Page 28 to replace webbing bands.

4. Check that springs [2] are tied securely together with twine [3].

If the springs are not tied securely they must be tied. Go to Page 33 to tie springs.

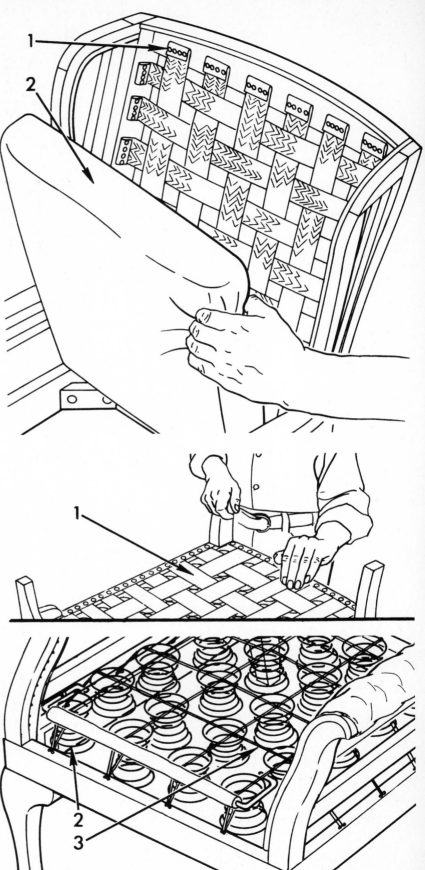

▶ **Inspecting Sagless Spring Support**

1. Check that sagless springs [3] are not bent or broken.

2. Check that springs [3] are securely attached to clips [1].

3. Check that clips [1] are securely attached to frame.

If springs or clips are defective, they must be replaced. Go to Page 26 to replace springs and clips.

4. Check that springs [3] are securely tied together with twine [2] or wire clips.

If springs are not securely tied together, they must be tied together. Go to Page 27 to tie springs.

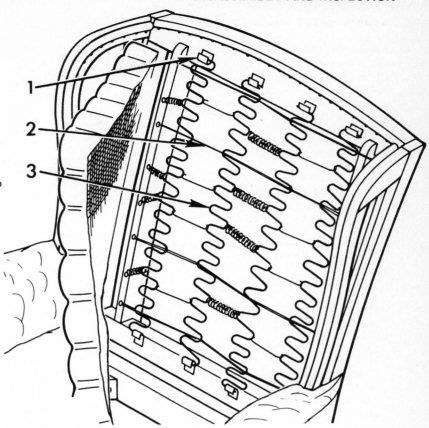

▶ **Inspecting Arms and Wings**

The arms and wings usually consist of cotton padding [1] supported by webbing bands [2] or cardboard [3].

1. Check that cotton padding [1] is not worn or deteriorating.

If cotton padding is worn or deteriorating, it must be replaced.

2. Carefully remove cotton padding [1].

3. Check that webbing bands [2] are not worn, torn or deteriorating.

If webbing bands are worn, torn or deteriorating, they must be replaced. Go to Page 28 to replace webbing bands.

4. Check that cardboard [3] is not torn or damaged.

If cardboard is torn or damaged, it must be replaced with a piece of cardboard of the same size and thickness.

5. Go to Page 46 to install cotton padding.

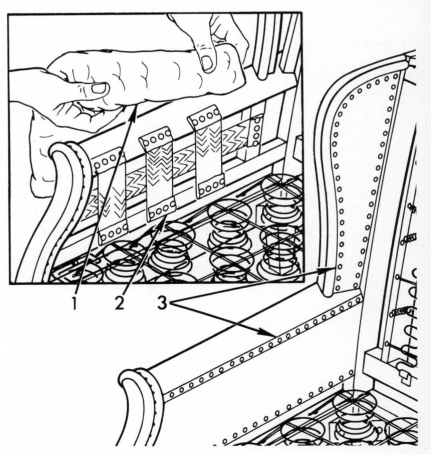

▶ Removing Sagless Springs and Clips

When removing sagless springs and clips, remove only the clips that need replacing or the clips holding the damaged springs.

The twine, wire or springs holding the sagless springs together must be removed before the clips or springs can be removed.

Be sure to force tacks in the direction of the wood grain.

1. Using hammer and screwdriver or ripping tool, remove tacks [3] holding twine [4] to frame. Remove twine.

2. Using pliers, remove all wire clips [5] and springs [6] holding springs together.

Before removing clips, mark the location of clips to aid in installing new clips.

3. Pry clip [1] from frame. Remove all tacks from clip.

4. Pry lip [2] open. Remove clip [1] from spring.

5. Repeat Steps 3 and 4 to remove all damaged clips and springs.

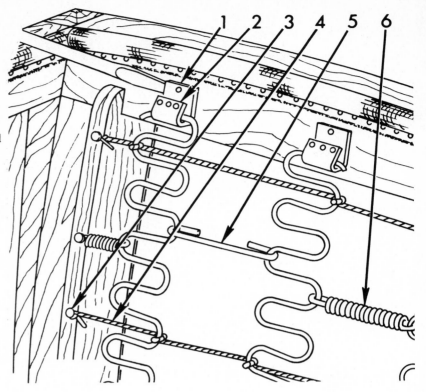

▶ Installing Sagless Springs and Clips

To insure that you receive the correct replacement parts, take the old springs, clips and nails to a reupholstery shop.

Be sure to have the springs cut to the correct length. Also, have their ends bent correctly.

All clips must be installed before the springs are installed.

Be sure to install clips at marks made when old clips were removed.

1. Place clip [2] at marked position. Using hammer drive one tack [1] through hole in clip into frame.

Repeat Step 1 until all clips are installed.

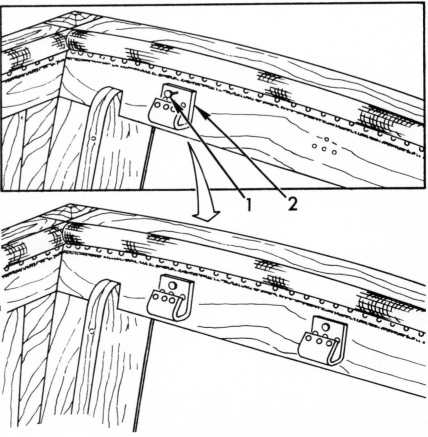

Installing Sagless Springs and Clips

If installing springs on a back, stretch the springs from bottom to top.

If installing springs on a seat, stretch the springs from back to front.

If the clip has three holes, drive nails through the two outer holes only. Do not drive three nails through the lip into the frame because this may split the rail.

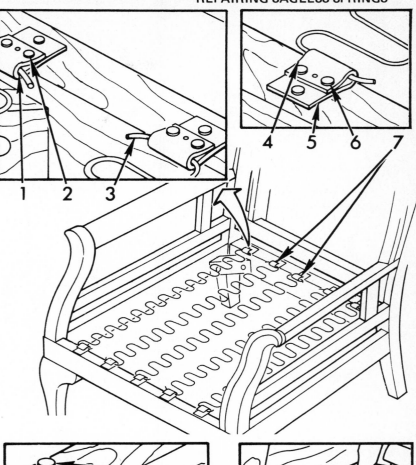

When installing springs, be sure to alternate the direction of the bent ends [7].

2. Place end of spring [3] into lip [1]. Using hammer, drive nails [2] through lip holes into frame.

3. Pull spring [3] to opposite clip [5]. Place end of spring into lip [4]. Using hammer, drive required nails [6] through lip holes into frame.

Repeat Steps 2 and 3 until all springs are installed.

▶ **Tying Sagless Springs**

After the springs are attached to the frame, they must be tied together with twine. Tie the springs at about five places.

Slip tacks are tacks that are driven 1/2 their length into the frame. They are installed on opposite rails. Center them on a row of arcs.

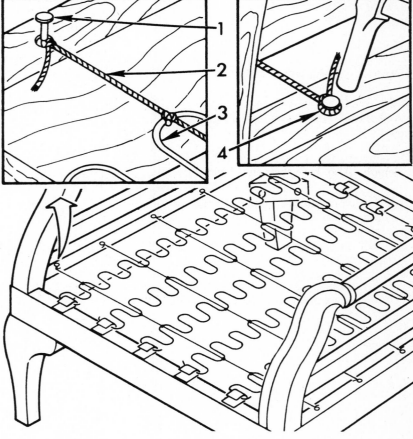

1. Drive required number of slip tacks [1, 4] into frame.

2. Tie one end of twine [2] to one slip tack [1]. Drive tack completely into frame.

3. Pull twine tight to first arc [3]. While holding twine tight, tie twine to arc.

Repeat Step 3 until all arcs in row are tied.

4. Pull twine tight to slip tack [4]. While holding twine tight, wrap twine around tack. Drive tack completely into frame. Cut and remove excess twine.

Repeat Steps 2 through 4 for remaining lengths of twine.

▶ **Removing Old Webbing Bands**

The old webbing bands must be removed before new webbing bands can be installed.

If the back has a polyurethane foam padding, remove the padding from the back.

If the back or seat has coil springs, they will be sewn or clipped to the bands. The webbing bands and springs should be removed as one unit.

Before removing the twine holding the springs to the frame, measure and record the following:

- Height of springs when tied
- Distance between springs and between springs and frame when tied

The twine holding the springs at their correct height and position must be removed.

Be sure to force the tacks in the direction of the wood grain.

1. Using hammer and screwdriver, remove all tacks [1] holding twine [2] to frame. Remove all twine from springs.

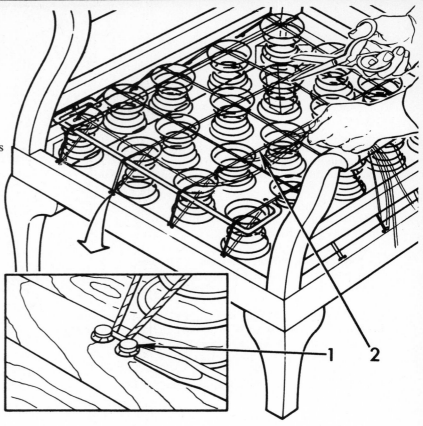

Removing Old Webbing Bands

Before removing old webbing bands, be sure to mark the location of each band as an aid in installing new bands.

All tacks holding one end of each band to the frame will be exposed. Some tacks holding the opposite end will be covered by the folded end of the band.

2. Remove all tacks [1] holding webbing bands [2] to frame. Remove all webbing bands with coil springs attached.

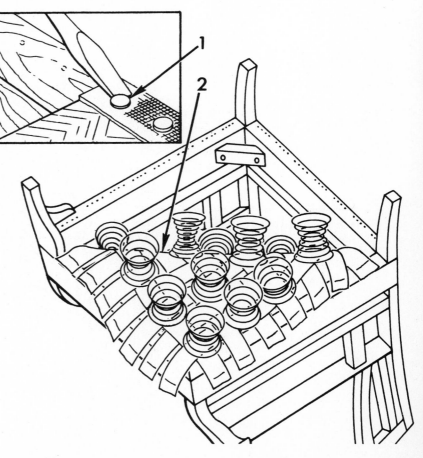

► Installing Webbing Bands

Webbing bands are installed on a frame by hand or with a webbing stretcher. The method of installation which you should use depends upon the style of the frame. First read Pages 29 through 30 to determine the proper method for your furniture. Then go to the following sections for a description of the procedures:

Stretching Bands With Webbing Stretcher, Page 30
Stretching Bands By Hand, Page 32

► Installing Webbing Bands On Backs

For all styles of backs except curved or barrel backs, the bottom-to-top webbing bands are stretched with a webbing stretcher. The side-to-side bands are woven through the bottom-to-top bands and stretched by hand until tight.

Curved [1] or barrel back chairs are chairs whose backs form extreme curves. The bottom-to-top bands are stretched with a webbing stretcher. The side-to-side bands are stretched by hand until they just touch the back of the bottom-to-top bands. They are NOT woven through the bottom-to-top bands.

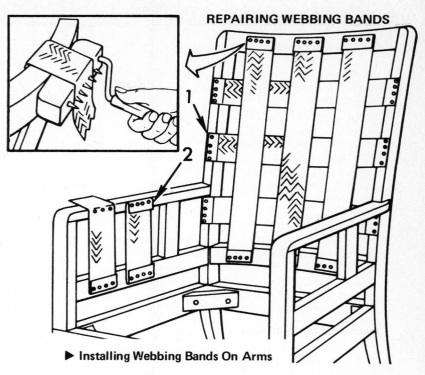

REPAIRING WEBBING BANDS

► Installing Webbing Bands On Arms

All arm bands [2] are stretched by hand only. If the arm has both bottom-to-top bands and front-to-back bands, install the bottom-to-top bands first.

► Installing Webbing Bands On Seats

For all seats except scoop seats, Page 30, and saddle seats the front-to-back bands are installed by using a webbing stretcher. The side-to-side bands are also installed by using a webbing stretcher. Be sure to weave the bands through the front-to-back bands.

A saddle seat [1] is curved downward on its front and back rails. The front-to-back bands are installed by using a webbing stretcher. The side-to-side bands are stretched by hand. These bands are NOT woven through the front-to-back bands. They are pulled tight enough to barely touch the bottom of the front-to-back bands.

When installing the side-to-side bands, do not pull them tight enough to distort the front-to-back bands.

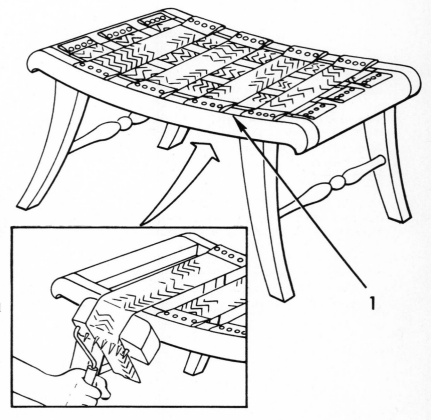

REPAIRING WEBBING BANDS

Installing Webbing Bands on Seats

A scoop seat [1], sometimes called a sag seat, is curved downward at its front rail. All the webbing bands are stretched by hand only. All the bands are allowed to sag slightly.

When installing webbing bands on a scoop seat, the bands must not be stretched too tightly or the seat will be uncomfortable. The bands must not sag too much or the seat will be difficult to rise from.

The middle front-to-back band is installed first with its correct amount of sag. The middle side-to-side band is installed next. It is allowed to sag until it just touches the top of the middle front-to-back band.

The remaining front-to-back bands are now installed. These bands are alternately placed under and over the side-to-side band. Each band is allowed to sag until it just touches the side-to-side band.

The remaining side-to-side bands are installed last. Each band is woven through the front-to-back bands. Each band is allowed to sag until it just touches the front-to-back bands.

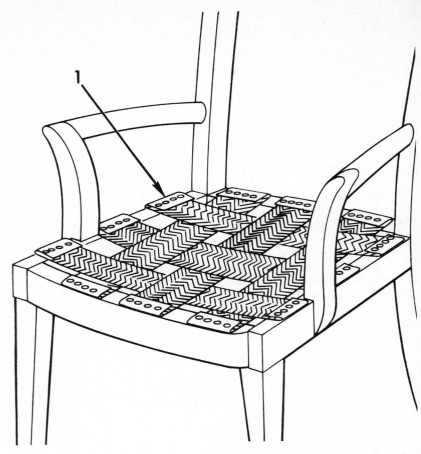

▶ **Stretching Bands With Webbing Stretcher**

If stretching all bands with webbing stretcher, stretch the front-to-back bands first. Then stretch the side-to-side bands.

To protect the front rail from being damaged by the webbing stretcher, stretch the bands from the front rail to the back rail.

Begin with center band and work toward edge bands.

Always install bands at marks made when old bands were removed.

1. Fold approximately 1-inch of end of band [2]. Place folded end at outer edge of rail.

When driving tacks into rail, be sure tacks are driven no closer than 1/8-inch from edges of rail. Be sure tacks are staggered to prevent splitting the rail.

2. Using tack hammer, drive seven tacks [1] through band into rail.

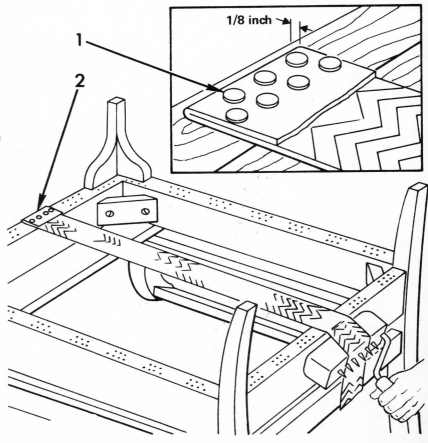

1/8 inch

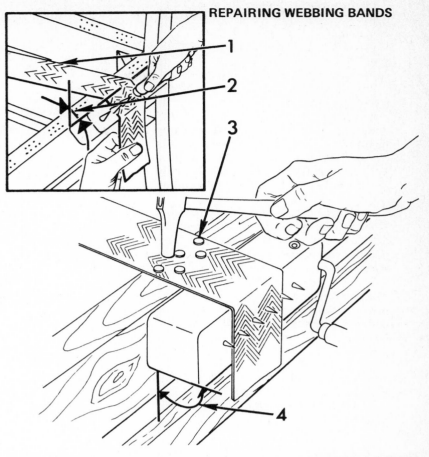

Stretching Bands With Webbing Stretcher

3. Pull band to opposite rail.

4. Place webbing stretcher at 45° angle [2] to rail. Pull webbing band [1] until all slack is removed from band. Force band over stretcher prongs.

Be sure webbing band is perpendicular to rail before forcing webbing stretcher to 90° angle.

5. Force and hold stretcher at 90° angle [4] with rail.

Be sure tacks are driven no closer than 1/8-inch from edges of rail. Be sure tacks are staggered to prevent splitting the rail. Be sure tacks are driven into rail in the sequence shown [3].

The two tacks on the edge of the band must be driven in the rail with the head of each tack even with the edge of the band.

6. Drive five tacks [3] through band into rail.

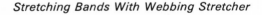

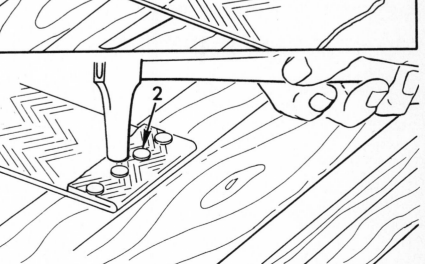

Stretching Bands With Webbing Stretcher

7. Remove webbing stretcher. Cut band [1] approximately 1-inch beyond edge of rail.

8. Fold end of band over tacks.

9. Drive four tacks [2] through band into rail.

Bands must not be stretched too tightly. If stretched too tightly, the frame or bands may be damaged or the tacks may pull from the rail.

To check that bands are stretched correctly, press down on band. Band should flex slightly. If band does not flex slightly, remove tacks and restretch the band.

Repeat Steps 1 through 9 until all bands are installed.

▶ **Stretching Bands By Hand**

Always install bands at marks made when old bands were removed.

1. Fold approximately 1-inch of end of band [2]. Place folded end at outer edge of rail.

When driving tacks into the rail, be sure tacks are driven no closer than 1/8-inch from the edges of the rail. Be sure tacks are staggered to prevent splitting the rail.

The two tacks on the edge of the band must be driven in the rail with the head of each tack even with the edge of the band.

2. Using tack hammer, drive seven tacks [1] through webbing into rail.

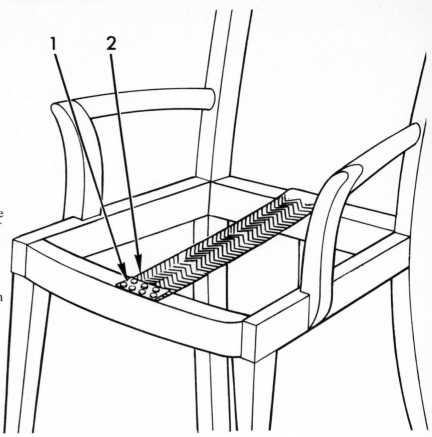

Stretching Bands By Hand

When pulling band to opposite rail, be sure band is stretched tight or allowed to sag, as required.

3. Pull band [1] to opposite rail.

4. While holding band [1] at desired tightness, drive five tacks through band into rail.

5. Cut band approximately 1-inch beyond edge of rail.

6. Fold end of band over tacks.

The two tacks on the edge of the band must be driven in the rail with the head of each tack even with the edge of the band.

7. Drive four tacks [2] through band into rail.

Repeat Steps 1 through 7 until all bands are installed.

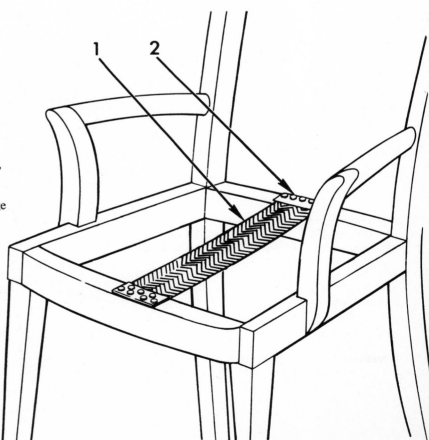

▶ **Removing Coil Springs**

Before removing any of the springs, measure and record the following:

● Height of the springs when tied

● Distance between springs and between springs and frame

If replacing both the springs and webbing bands, remove the twine holding the springs at the correct height. Then remove the webbing bands and springs as one unit. Go to Page 28 to remove webbing bands and springs together.

If removing an individual spring, remove the twine holding the spring in front-to-back row and side-to-side row. Do not remove any other twine unless necessary to untie the spring being removed.

Be sure to force tacks in the direction of the wood grain.

1. Using hammer and screwdriver, remove tacks [3] holding twine [2] to frame.

2. Remove twine [2] from all springs [1] in front-to-back and side-to-side rows.

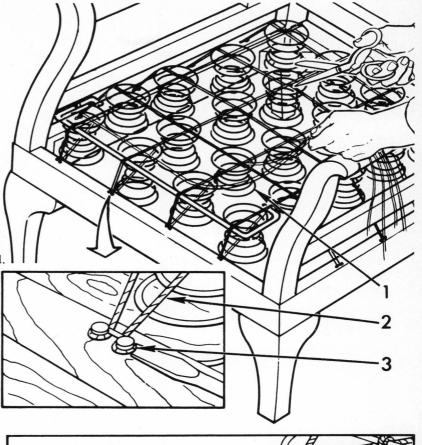

Removing Coil Springs

If the spring [3] being removed is attached to an edge wire [5], the twine [4] or clip holding the spring to the edge wire must be removed before the spring can be removed.

The springs may be attached to the webbing bands with twine [2] or clips [1].

If clips are used to hold the springs to the bands, remove only the clips holding the spring being removed.

CAUTION

If the springs are sewn to the webbing bands, generally only one piece of twine will be used. As a result, when the twine is cut to remove one spring, all the springs will become loose.

Therefore, as soon as the twine is cut, tie a knot in the free end of the twine to hold the remaining springs to the bands. This will prevent the springs from becoming loose.

If removing all springs, cut and remove the twine at each spring or remove all clips.

3. Cut and remove twine [2] holding spring to webbing bands. Remove spring.

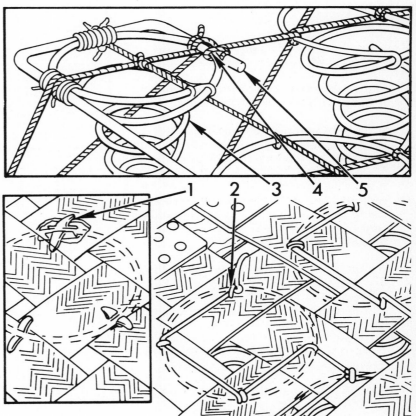

REPAIRING COIL SPRINGS

▶ **Attaching Springs To Webbing Bands**

When replacing springs, take the old springs to an upholstery shop to insure exact replacement.

If clips are used to attach springs to webbing bands, take the old clip to an upholstery shop to insure exact replacement. If replacing all springs, do not use clips; use twine to sew the springs to the webbing bands.

Springs are made with a top and bottom. The top of the spring has its tip [1] bent toward the center of the spring. Be sure to place the bottom of the spring against the webbing bands.

If replacing all springs, position each spring at its approximate position. After all springs are roughly arranged, they are sewn to the webbing bands at their exact position.

If replacing individual springs, place the spring at its exact position. Then sew the spring to the webbing bands.

If installing springs for spring edges, the springs must be bent before they are sewn to the webbing bands. Go to Page 39 to bend springs.

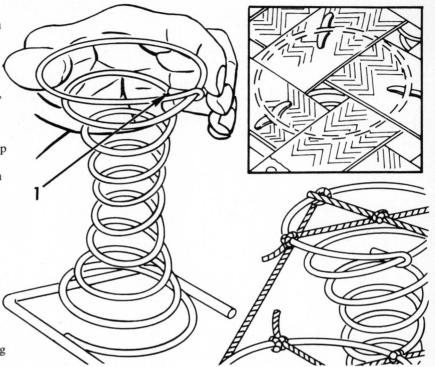

Attaching Springs To Webbing Bands

1.   Place spring [1] on webbing bands at desired location.

If attaching a spring with clips, use three clips to attach the spring to webbing bands.

If attaching springs with twine, use a double pointed straight upholsterer's needle and stitching twine to sew springs to webbing bands.

If installing all springs, be sure the twine is long enough to sew all the springs to the webbing bands. Begin stitching them to the bands at any corner spring. Be sure that the last stitch is next to another spring.

2.   Push needle up through webbing band as near bottom coil [1] as possible. Pull twine [2] through band until end of twine is approximately 1-inch from band.

3.   Push needle back through webbing band on inside of bottom coil [3] as near coil as possible. Pull all twine through band.

4.   Tie tight knot [4] at bottom of webbing.

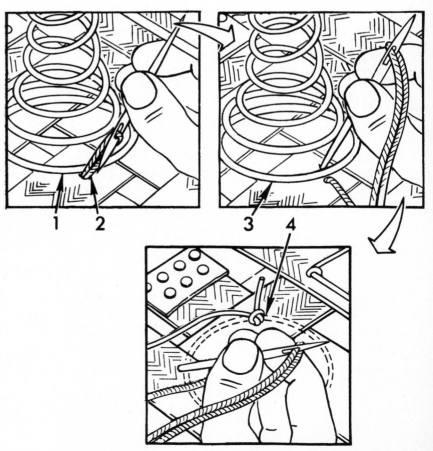

Attaching Springs To Webbing Bands

Each spring is sewn to the webbing bands with four stitches. Stitches should be spaced equally distant from each other around the bottom coil.

If installing all springs, the last stitch on each spring should be made near another spring so that one piece of twine can be used to stitch all the springs.

5. Push needle up through webbing at outside of coil [1]. Push needle back through webbing on inside of coil [2]. Pull twine tight.

Repeat Step 5 until all four stitches are made.

If installing all springs, repeat Step 5 until all springs are stitched to webbing bands.

After all springs are sewn to the bands, be sure to tie a tight knot in the loose end of the twine.

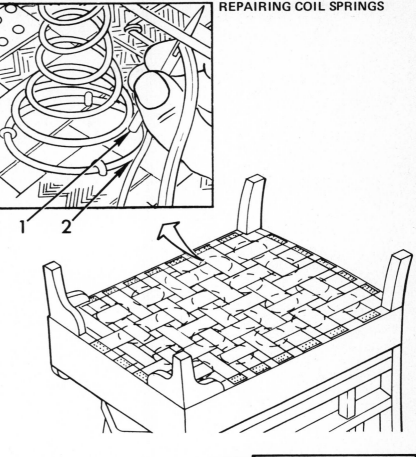

▶ Tying a Round Seat

After the springs are securely stitched to the webbing bands, the springs must be tied at their correct height and position.

Springs are tied in rows from back-to-front and side-to-side. Some chairs may also use diagonal ties.

In any direction, the springs are tied with two lengths of twine. The first length of twine [1] is simply looped around the top coils to position the springs at their desired height.

The second length of twine [2] is tied to the coils over the loops to hold the springs at their correct position and height.

Always tie the front-to-back rows first, then tie the side-to-side rows.

If tying all the rows, begin with the center row and work to the edge rows.

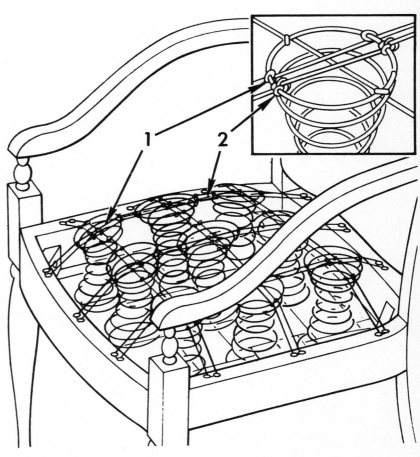

REPAIRING COIL SPRINGS

Tying a Round Seat

When tying the springs, be sure to tie them at the height measured when the springs were removed.

1. Measure distance from rail to rail. Multiply distance by 2. Cut twine at distance figured.

Slip tacks are tacks that are driven 1/2 their length into the frame. Slip tacks are driven at the center of the row of springs being tied. Be sure to use 12 oz or 14 oz tacks.

2. Drive one slip tack [1] in each opposite rail of row being tied.

3. Tie twine [2] to one slip tack [1]. Drive tack completely into rail.

When tying the springs, check the tack often. If tack begins to pull from the rail, drive another tack into rail with its head covering the head of the installed tack.

Tying a Round Seat

4. Connect all springs in one row by looping the twine around opposite sides of each top coil.

When adjusting springs to their correct height, be sure to keep them aligned in a straight row.

5. While pulling tightly on loose end of twine [1], compress each spring to its correct height.

6. While pulling twine [1] tightly, wrap twine around tack [2]. Drive tack completely into rail. Cut and remove excess twine.

A second length of twine must be tied to the springs to hold the springs at their correct height and position.

The second length of twine is installed like the first length, except that all loops made by first length are tied to the coils with the second length of twine.

Repeat Step 1 through 6 to tie second length of twine to springs.

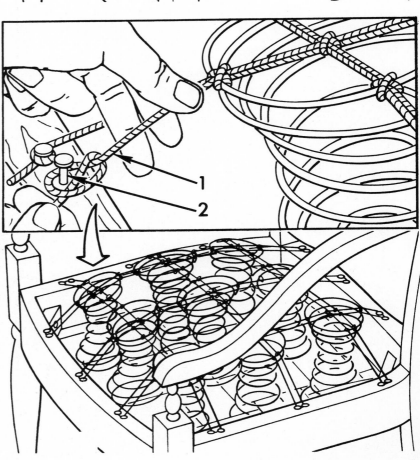

▶ **Tying a Flat Seat**

After the springs are sewn to the webbing bands, the springs must be tied at their correct height and position.

If installing springs for spring edges, the springs must be attached to the edge wire [1] before the seat can be tied. Go to Page 39 to attach springs to edge wire.

Springs are tied from back-to-front and side-to-side. Some chairs may also use diagonal ties.

In any direction, the springs are tied with two lengths of twine. The first length of twine [2] is looped around the coils to position the springs at their desired height.

The second length [3] is tied to the coils over the loops to hold the springs at their correct position and height.

Always tie the back-to-front rows first. Then tie the side-to-side rows.

If tying all rows, begin with the center row and work to the edge rows.

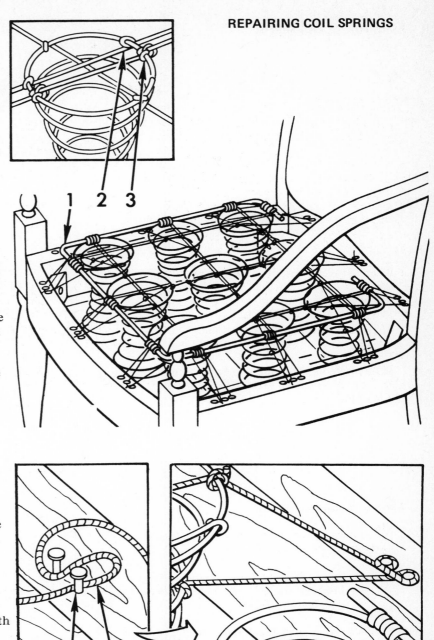

Tying a Flat Seat

When tying the springs, be sure to tie them at the height measured when the springs were removed.

1. Measure distance from rail to rail. Multiply distance by 3. Add 4 inches. Cut twine at distance figured.

Slip tacks are tacks that are driven 1/2 their length into the frame. They are driven at the center of the row of springs being tied.

Be sure to stagger slip tacks to prevent splitting the rail.

2. Drive two slip tacks [1] on opposite rails of row being tied.

When making a loop in the twine, be sure to allow approximately 20 inches on short end of twine.

3. Make loop [2] in twine approximately 20 inches from one end. Slide loop between tacks [1]. Fold loop over tacks. Pull twine tight.

4. Drive tacks [1] completely into rail.

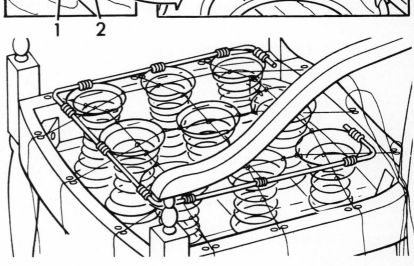

REPAIRING COIL SPRINGS

Tying a Flat Seat

5.   Loop twine [7] around third coil [6] from top on outer side of first spring. Loop twine around opposite top coil [5].

6.   Connect all springs [1] except last spring of row by looping the twine around opposite sides of each top coil.

7.   Loop twine around inner side of top coil [4] of last spring. Loop twine around third coil [3] from top of outer side.

When adjusting springs to their correct height, the outer edge of the first and last coil cannot be tied at its correct height.

8.   While pulling tightly on loose end of twine, adjust each spring to its correct height.

9.   While pulling twine tightly, wrap twine around two slip tacks [2]. Drive tacks completely into rail.

Tying a Flat Seat

The outer edges of the first and last springs must be tied with the excess twine.

10.   Compress and hold outer edge [2] of top coil at desired height. Using excess twine [3] tie outer edge at desired height.

11.   Pull twine to opposite side [1] of top coil. Tie twine to coil. Cut and remove excess twine.

Repeat Steps 10 and 11 for remaining outer coils.

A second length of twine must be tied to the springs to insure that springs remain at their correct height and position.

The second length of twine is installed like the first length, except that all loops made by first length are tied to the coils with the second length of twine.

Repeat Steps 1 through 11 to tie second length of twine to springs.

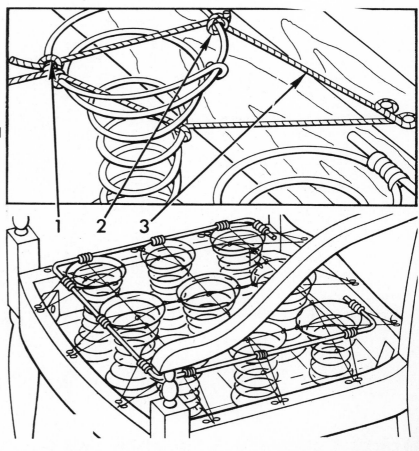

▶ Tying Spring Edges

If the seat on a chair has a spring edge [1], each coil spring around the edges of the seat must be bent into an oval shape [2].

When bending the springs, try to make all the springs the same shape to insure that the seat is smooth and uniform.

The top coil only of a spring should be bent into an oval. The tip [3] of the coil should be turned away from the spring edge [1].

1.   Bend top coil to oval shape [2].

After all springs around the edge of the seat are bent, the springs must be attached to the webbing bands.

When attaching the springs to the webbing bands, be sure the oval end is positioned to fit against the spring edge [1].

Go to Page 34 to attach springs to webbing bands.

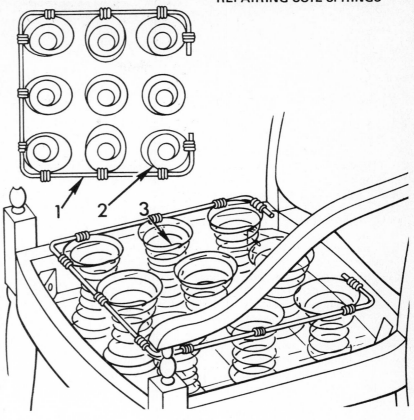

Tying Spring Edges

After all springs are attached to the webbing bands, the springs [2] around the edge of the seat must be attached to the spring edge [3].

The spring edge wire is a heavy gauge wire which is seldom damaged. The spring edge wire [3] may be attached to the springs [2] only or it may be attached to the frame in addition to the springs.

If the spring edge wire [3] was attached to the frame and has been removed, it must be attached to the frame before the springs [2] are attached to it.

The springs [2] can be fastened to the spring edge [3] with twine [4] or with clips [1]. Clips are easier and faster to install than twine.

2.   Attach springs [2] to spring edge [3].

After the springs are attached to the spring edge, the springs must be tied. The seats are tied like a flat seat. Go to Page 37 to tie springs.

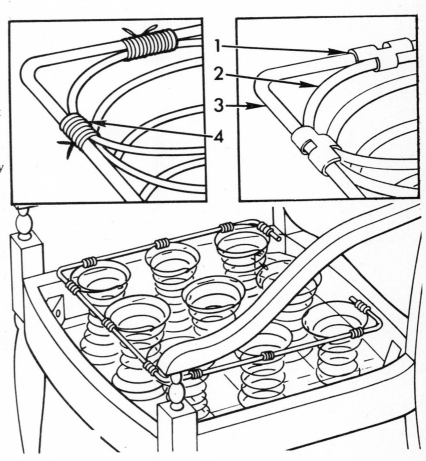

Coil springs, sagless springs or polyurethane foam must be covered with burlap to prevent the padding from being forced between the springs.

If old burlap cover can be reused, go to Step 4. Read notes before Step 4.

If old burlap cover can be used as a pattern, go to Step 3.

If old cover cannot be used as a pattern, the seat or back must be measured and the burlap cut into a rectangle at the measured size. Continue.

When measuring the seat or back, use a flexible cloth tape measure. Measure the contour of the seat or back.

1. For back, measure distance from top rail [1] to bottom rail [2]. Measure distance from side rail to side rail. Add 2 inches to distances measured.

2. For seat, measure distance from front rail [4] to back rail [3]. Measure distance from side rail to side rail. Add 2 inches to distances measured.

3. Cut new burlap to correct size.

If installing burlap cover on a back, attach the cover to the top rail [1] first. Then pull the cover to the bottom rail [2] and attach it to the bottom rail. The sides are tacked after the top and bottom edges are tacked.

If installing burlap cover on a seat, attach the cover to the front rail [4] first. Then pull the cover to the back rail [3] and attach it to the back rail. The sides are tacked after the front and back edges are tacked.

If installing a new cover not cut from a pattern, the cover must be cut to fit around the obstructions [5].

4. Position cover on back or seat.

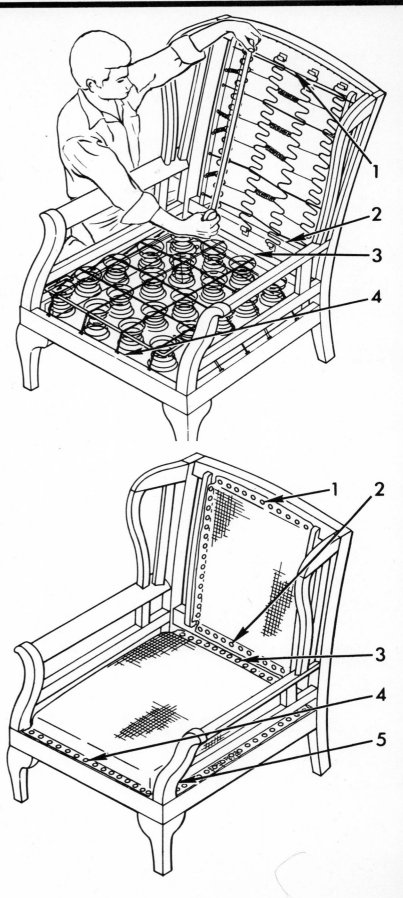

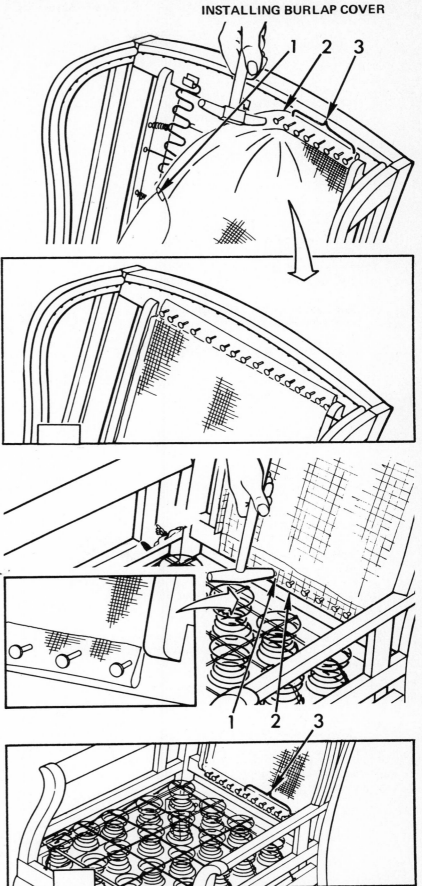

When installing the cover, use 4 oz tacks. Drive the tacks into the rails recorded when the cover was removed.

5. Fold edge [1] of burlap approximately 1/2-inch.

A slip tack is a tack that is driven 1/2 its length into the rail.

6. Drive one slip tack through folded edge [1] into center of rail [2].

Slip tacks should be spaced approximately 1 inch apart.

7. While pulling cover tightly to one corner, drive slip tacks [3] through folded edge [1] into rail [2].

Repeat Step 7 for opposite corner.

When pulling cover to opposite rail, pull cover tightly but do not pull cover tight enough to compress springs or foam.

8. Pull cover to opposite rail. Fold approximately 1/2-inch of edge [2].

9. Drive one slip tack through folded edge [2] into center of rail [1].

Slip tacks should be spaced approximately 1 inch apart.

10. While pulling cover tightly to one corner, drive slip tacks [3] through folded edge [2] into rail [1].

Repeat Step 10 for opposite corner.

INSTALLING BURLAP COVER

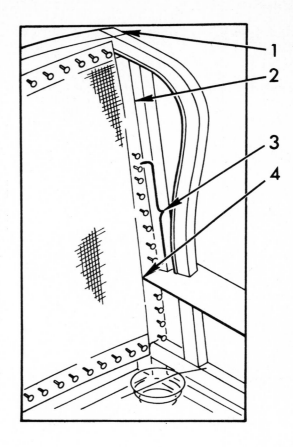

11.   Pull one side edge of cover to side rail [1].
      Fold approximately 1/2-inch of edge [2].

12.   Drive one slip tack through folded edge [2]
      into center of rail [1].

If rail has no obstructions, go to Step 16, below.

If rail has an obstruction [4], continue.

13.   Pull cover tightly to obstruction [4].

Drive tacks into rail as near to the obstruction as
possible. Do not tack cover to the obstruction.

14.   Drive slip tacks [3] through folded edge [2]
      until obstruction [4] is reached.

15.   Cut cover to fit around obstruction [4].

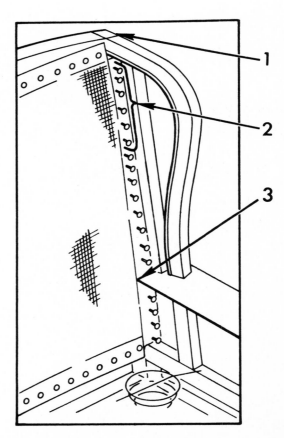

16.   Pull cover tightly to corner [1].

17.   Drive slip tacks [2] through folded edge into
      rail.

If side rail has no obstruction, repeat Steps 16
and 17 for opposite corner.

If side rail has an obstruction [3], repeat Steps 13
through 17 to install cover between obstruction
and corner.

18.   Repeat Steps 11 through 17 for remaining
      side of cover.

19.   Check that cover is smooth and even.

If cover is not smooth and even, remove necessary
slip tacks and adjust cover until it is smooth
and even. Replace slip tacks.

20.   Drive all slip tacks completely into frame.

▶ **Installing Foam Padding**

If old moss or hair padding was removed, do not install the old padding even if it is in usable condition. Instead, replace it with polyurethane foam.

To install the foam, it must be cut to the correct size and laid into position. The weight of the foam will hold it in position until the muslin cover is installed.

The thickness of the new padding is determined from the thickness of the old padding.

If replacing a coil spring back with foam, use 4-inch foam.

Use a hand saw or electric carving knife to cut the foam to the correct size.

If the old padding has kept its shape it can be used as a pattern. If it cannot be used as a pattern, the area where the padding is to be installed must be measured and the foam cut to shape.

1. Cut foam [1] to correct size. Place foam at desired location.

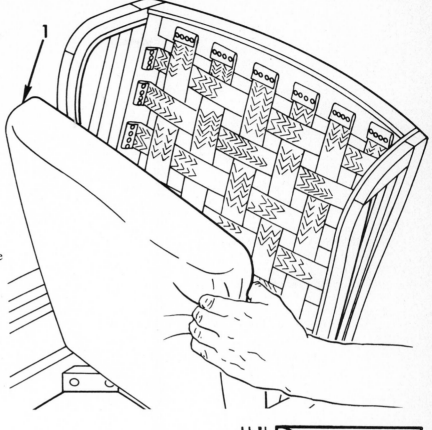

▶ **Installing Edge Roll on Wood Edges**

An edge roll is needed on wood edges to soften the edges and hold the padding in position.

If edge roll has not been removed, it must be removed. After removing edge roll, keep the roll to use as a guide to cut new roll to correct length.

Be sure to force tacks in the direction of the wood grain.

1. Remove all tacks [2] holding edge roll [3] to rail [1]. Remove edge roll.

2. Using old edge roll as a guide, measure and cut needed lengths of edge roll.

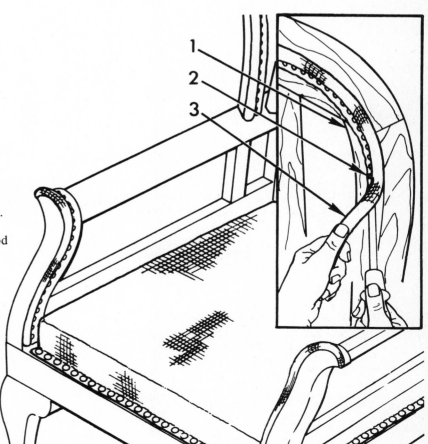

INSTALLING PADDING

Installing Edge Roll on Wood Edges

If edge roll must be installed at a corner, butt [2] the edge roll together at the corner.

If edge roll must be installed at an obstruction, tack the edge roll to the obstruction.

If edge roll must be installed on curves, pleat [1] the roll to follow the curve.

3.   Place edge roll [3] at rail edge [4]. Position edge roll so that it overhangs outside of rail edge by approximately 1/4-inch.

When installing straight pieces of edge roll, pull the roll to make a smooth, even surface.

When driving tacks, be sure to stagger the tacks to prevent splitting the rail.

Begin at one end of roll and work toward the opposite end.

4.   Drive required tacks through flat back of edge roll [3] into rail [5].

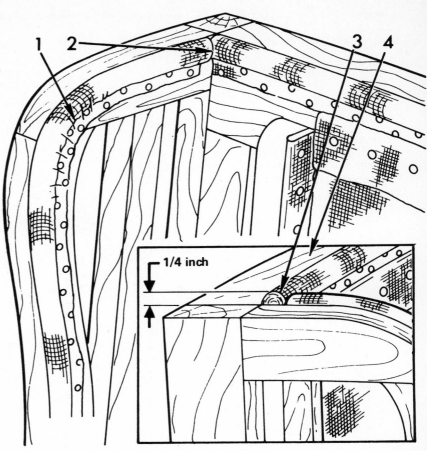

▶ **Installing Edge Roll on Spring Edges**

An edge roll is needed on spring edge wires to cushion the hardness of the wire.

If edge roll has not been removed, it must be removed. After removing edge roll, keep the roll to use as a guide to cut new roll to correct length.

1.   Using razor blade, cut and remove all stitches [1] holding edge roll [4] to burlap. Cut and remove all stitches [2] holding edge roll to spring edge wire [3]. Remove edge roll.

2.   Using old edge roll as a guide, cut needed lengths of edge roll.

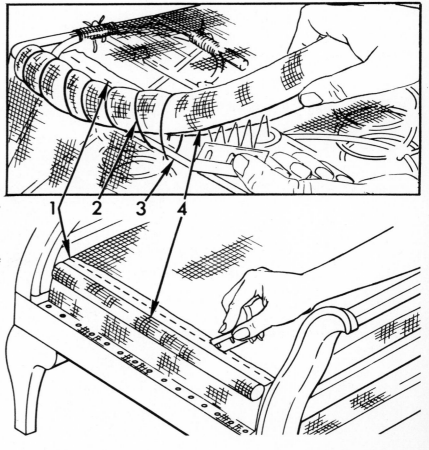

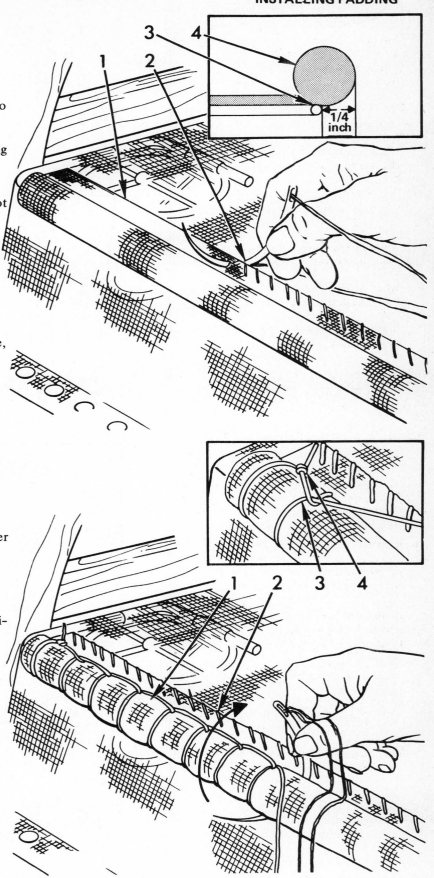

Installing Edge Roll on Spring Edges

If edge roll must be installed at a corner, butt two pieces of edge roll together at the corner.

A 5-inch curved upholsterer's needle and stitching twine are used to sew the edge roll to the burlap cover.

When threading the needle be sure to make a knot at end of thread.

3. Place edge roll [4] at edge wire [3]. Position edge roll so that it overhangs outside of edge wire by approximately 1/4-inch.

Use back stitches to sew edge roll to burlap.

4. Using curved needle [2] and stitching twine, sew flat edge [1] of edge roll to burlap.

Installing Edge Roll on Spring Edges

5. Push needle down through stitches [2] in edge roll [1] into burlap. Push needle under edge wire and back through burlap as near front of edge roll as possible.

6. Tie a tight knot [4] in twine.

Remaining stitches [3] should be placed approximately 1-inch apart.

7. Push needle down through stitches in roll into burlap. Push needle under edge wire and back through burlap as near front of edge roll as possible.

8. Push needle under twine. Pull twine tight to form stitch [3].

Repeat Steps 7 and 8 until all but the last stitch is made.

Repeat Step 5 for last stitch.

INSTALLING PADDING

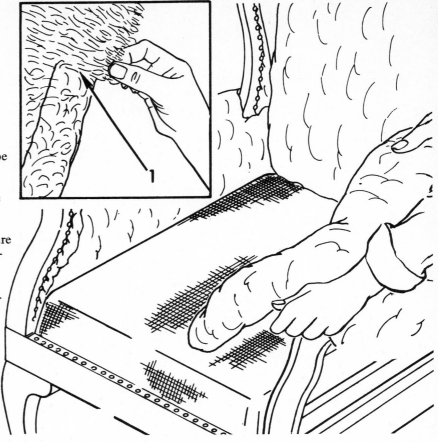

▶ **Installing Cotton Padding**

Cotton padding is the last layer of padding to be placed on a seat, back, or arm.

This padding is cut or pulled to the correct size and laid on the lower levels of padding.

If cutting the material to the correct size, be sure to feather the edges [1] to leave a smooth contour without sharp edges.

1. Cut or pull cotton padding to correct size. Place padding at desired location.

■■ INSTALLING MUSLIN COVER ■■■

A muslin cover is simply a piece of common muslin fabric which is fitted snugly over the padded parts of furniture and tacked in place. It is used on the arms, backs and seats of furniture.

Because it is an extra operation in the manufacture of furniture and would add to its cost, very few pieces are made with a muslin cover. You may not find a muslin cover on your furniture to use as a pattern for cutting and installing a new one. However, they are easy to make and install and it would be well worth your time to do so. It is a particularly good idea for the amatuer upholsterer to add a muslin cover for the following reasons:

● It provides valuable practice for installing the upholstery itself.

● It holds the padding securely in place so that the final appearance of the furniture is improved. A better looking and longer lasting reupholstery job is almost sure to result.

The main purpose of a muslin cover is to provide a smooth, even surface for installing the top cover.

There are only a few general guidelines which you should follow for installing a muslin cover.

First, you must select the rails to which you will tack the muslin cover. In most cases, it is best to use the same rails as used for tacking the top cover. However, you may use a different side of the rail for tacking the muslin cover so that the muslin cover does NOT interfere with installing the top cover. So remember:

● The top cover must be installed over the muslin cover. Do not tack the muslin cover to a rail that will prevent installation of the top cover.

● Tack the muslin cover as near to the padding as possible so that you leave as much rail surface as possible for tacking the top cover.

Install muslin covers in this sequence: inside back, inside arms and seat.

The inside back cover is tacked first to the top rail, then the bottom rail and, last, the side rails.

The inside arm cover is tacked first to the armboard, then the arm liner, the arm stump and arm slat.

The seat cover is tacked first to the front rail, then the back rail and, last, the side rails.

The procedures for installing any muslin cover, whether it is for a back, arms or seat are as follows:

1. Select the rails and sides of rails to which muslin is to be tacked.

2. Using old top cover as a rough pattern, cut a piece of muslin. Cut the muslin so that the threads run perpendicular to the edges.

3. Center the muslin on the back, arm or seat.

4. Drive one slip tack [3] into the center of the rail.

5. Pull muslin to one corner. Drive one slip tack [1] into the corner.

6. Drive one slip tack [2] between corner tack and center tack.

7. Pull muslin to other corner. Drive one slip tack [5] into corner. Drive one slip tack [4] between corner tack and center tack.

8. Repeat Steps 4 through 7 for opposite rail [6].

9. Repeat Steps 4 through 7 for side rails.

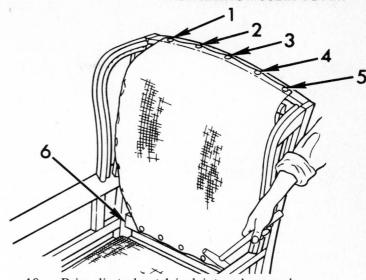

10. Drive slip tacks at 1-inch intervals around edge of fabric.

11. Check that muslin cover and padding is smooth and even. Remove tacks and adjust cover as necessary.

12. Drive all slip tacks completely into rails.

13. Fold and tack any excess material at corners.

INSTALLING NEW TOP COVER

▶ **Measuring and Estimating**

After all repairs have been made and the muslin cover installed, the top cover sections can be installed.

When each section of the old cover was removed it should have been labeled. Now each section must be pressed and laid on the floor to estimate the amount of material needed.

Welting strips that are sewn to the top cover sections must be removed from the sections. When removing the strips, observe and record the location of the strip on the sections to aid in machine sewing the new top cover sections.

1. Using single edge razor blade, cut and remove stitches holding welting strip to cover section. Remove welting strip.

Any machine sewn seams should still be sewn in the individual top cover sections. When cutting the stitches, observe and record the location of seams to aid in machine sewing seams for new top cover sections.

2. Using single edge razor blade, cut and remove stitches forming seams.

The section must be pressed before it can be used as a pattern.

3. Using iron, press section until it is flat and free of wrinkles.

Repeat Steps 1 through 3 until all sections are pressed.

The cover sections must be laid out and measured to estimate the amount of material needed.

Lay the sections on the floor as you will lay them on the new material. The floor area where the sections are laid should be 54 inches wide and as long as necessary to lay and arrange all the sections.

Page 48 shows how to lay out all the old top cover sections.

After the sections are arranged on the floor, the length of the area must be measured.

4. Measure length of area. Increase length to next higher yard.

This is the length of material to be purchased.

INSTALLING NEW TOP COVER

► **Layout and Cutting of New Material**

The old cover sections must be laid on the new material and the new material cut to size.

If using material with a pattern, the sections should be arranged to allow the patterns to match.

If using material with a nap, the sections must be arranged so that nap runs from back-to-front on the seat cover and from top-to-bottom on all other sections.

If the material has no pattern or nap, the material should be arranged in such a way to use the least material.

When arranging the old sections on the material, place the band strips and box strips across the top of the material.

Lay the widest sections on the material below the strips, and work to the end with the narrower sections.

Section below shows how to layout the top cover sections.

1. Arrange all old top cover sections on new material.

After all the sections are arranged, the welting strips can be arranged.

If the material has no nap or pattern, the welting can be arranged lengthwise on the extra material.

If the material has nap or a pattern, the welting strips must be laid on the bias. Arrange the welting to use the least amount of material.

When arranging the welting strips on the material, the strips will still be sewn. Lay the full length of the strips on the material and allow 1-3/4 inches for the width of each strip.

2. Arrange all welting strips on new material.

As you draw the outline of each old section, remove the section and label the new material to identify it.

3. Using chalk, draw outline of each piece on new cover material. Label each piece.

4. Using scissors, cut all pieces from new material.

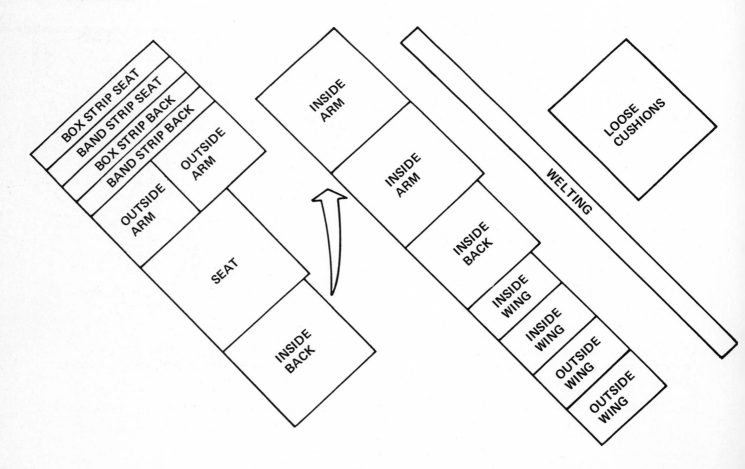

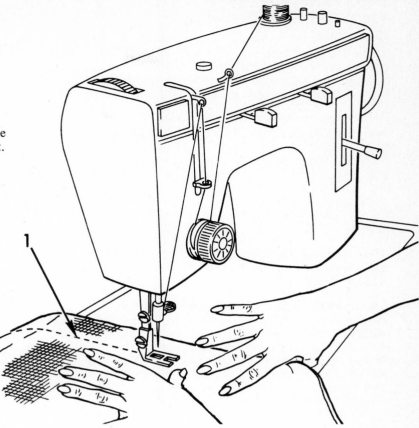

▶ **Machine Sewing**

After all the sections are cut, any machine sewn seams must be made. The seams are sewn into the sections where recorded when the seams were cut.

If using a home sewing machine, set the machine to sew its largest stitch.

Make all necessary seams in one section before sewing seams in another section.

1.   Using sewing machine, sew all necessary seams [1] in one section of top cover material.

Repeat Step 1 until all seams are sewn in all sections.

Machine Sewing

The welting strips must be made and then sewn to the top cover sections where recorded.

When making welting strips, use a sewing machine with a zipper foot.

1.   Place 5/32-inch welt cord [1] in center of 1-3/4 inch strip [2]. Fold strip over cord and align edges [3].

Before sewing, be sure that cord is in center of strip. Do not sew the material against the cord. Leave approximately 1/4-inch of material between cord and seam.

2.   Using sewing machine, sew welting strip.

Repeat Steps 1 and 2 until all welting strips are sewn.

The welting strips must be sewn to the top cover sections where recorded when the welting strips were removed.

When sewing the welting strips, stretch the strip to be sure that edge of the cover is smooth and even.

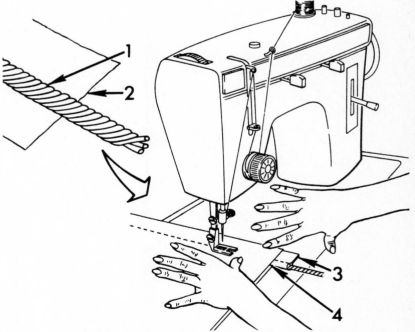

3.   Using sewing machine, sew welting strip [4] to top cover section.

Repeat Step 4 until all welting strips are sewn to top cover sections.

INSTALLING NEW TOP COVER

▶ **Blind Stitching**

Blind stitching is a technique for making the stitches holding a seam together nearly invisible. They are hand sewn stitches which are used to join top cover sections at edges which cannot be machine sewn or tacked in place.

For example, the back cover will ordinarily be the last top section to be installed. Typically, it will be blind tacked along the top edge [1], then joined to other cover sections with blind stitching at the sides [2] and, last, fastened to the underside of the back rail [3] with tacks.

A curved upholsterer's needle [7] is required to make a blind stitch. A 3-inch needle is adequate. Stout No. 40 thread of a color which matches the top cover may be used for stitching. Thread the needle with a double length of thread. Start the stitch so that the knot [4] is hidden.

The technique of blind stitching is to make the visible part [5] of the stitch very small. The stitching thread is looped over only 2 or 3 threads of the top cover material. To further conceal the stitches, they are spaced only at approximately 1/2-inch intervals [6] along the seam. Pull the seam together tightly as you progress from the top to the bottom of the seam.

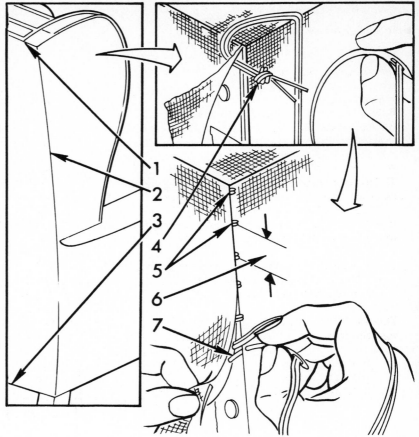

▶ **Blind Tacking**

Blind tacking is used to install one edge of some cover sections to the frame.

By using a cardboard strip and tacking through the back of the cover, a smooth edge can be formed where two top cover sections meet.

1. Place cover [1] at rail with face side down. Adjust edge of cover until it is at desired position.

2. Using tack hammer, drive tacks [2] 2 to 3 inches apart along edge of cover to hold it in place. Be sure cover is even and uniform along entire edge.

3. Place and hold cardboard strip [4] over edge of cover at rail. Using tack hammer, drive one slip tack [3] through cardboard into center of rail.

4. Pull cover [1] tightly to one corner. Drive required slip tacks through cardboard into rail.

5. Pull cover [1] tightly to opposite corner. Drive required slip tacks through cardboard into rail.

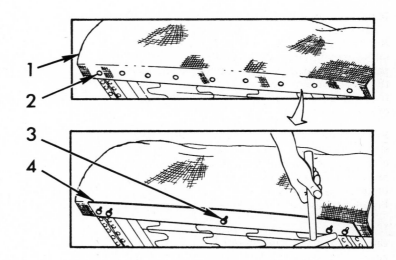

The cover must be even and uniform along the entire length of the cardboard strip.

If cover is not even and uniform, remove slip tacks and repeat Steps 1 through 5.

After cover is even and uniform, slip tacks must be driven completely into the rail.

6. Using tack hammer, drive all slip tacks completely into rail.

► **Installing Welting Strips**

If welting strips are needed between sections of the top cover material and are not sewn to the sections, they must be tacked to the frame.

Before beginning to tack a welting strip to the frame, be sure the strip is long enough to cover the entire length of frame to be covered.

When installing a welting strip, begin at one end. The welting strip must be installed at the position recorded when the welting strip was removed.

If welting must fit on a curved surface, pleat the welting strip while installing.

1. Place welting strip [2] at recorded position. Using tack hammer, drive one tack [1] through flat edge of strip into frame.

The welting strip must be pulled tightly to prevent the strip from gathering while tacking.

2. While pulling strip [2] tightly away from first tack, drive required tacks [1] through flat edge into rail.

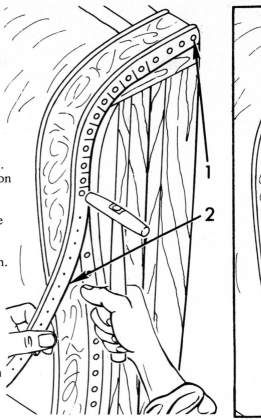

► **Installing Covers on Loose Cushions**

Recovering loose cushions involves many of the same tasks found in dressmaking: making patterns, cutting the fabric and fitting and sewing the pieces. There are several different approaches to recovering, depending upon the construction of the cushion.

Spring cushions. If the cushion is damaged, it should be replaced with polyurethane foam. It is easier for the amatuer to work with foam than to repair damaged springs. A good foam cushion can be perfectly serviceable and comfortable. Read Page 43 for instructions for cutting foam.

If the old spring cushion is in good condition, it can be recovered. One method is to leave the cushion completely intact and simply cover it with the new material. Of course, if there are welting strips around the edges, they must first be removed. You may cut the fabric and remove the cord only or you may remove the entire strip. Be sure not to damage the seams between the sections of the cover. Read Page 56 for instructions for sewing the new welting strips.

If there are any buttons in the cushion, they must be removed and replaced. You may wish to bring the buttons to an upholstery shop for recovering.

Another approach to recovering spring cushions is remove the old cover and use it as a pattern for making the new cover.

Foam cushions. Many times you will find that by the time the upholstery needs replacing, the foam has also deteriorated. If this is the case, replace the foam. Read Page 43 for instructions for cutting foam.

Use the old cover as a pattern for cutting and sewing the new cover. Read Page 56 for instructions for sewing welting strips. Buttons can be taken to an upholstery shop for recovering.

Stuffed cushions. Down, kapok, dacron, shredded foam or other materials are used to stuff cushions. Use the old cover as a pattern for making the new cover and transfer the stuffing to it. If welting strips are required, read Page 56 for instructions for making them. Buttons can be taken to an upholstery shop for recovering.

INSTALLING NEW TOP COVER

▶ **Installing Cover Sections**

Before installing any of the top cover sections a 1/2-inch layer of cotton padding must be installed over the muslin cover. This layer gives the chair its final form and covers any small defects in the muslin cover.

Install the new top cover sections in the following order:

- Seat Cover, Page 52
- Inside Wing Cover, if required, Page 57
- Inside Arm Cover, Page 58
- Inside Back Cover, Page 60
- Outside Wing Cover, if required, Page 63
- Outside Arm Cover, Page 64
- Outside Back Cover, Page 67

If installing a tufted back, be sure to read Installing a Tufted Back, Page 70, before continuing.

If installing a channel back, be sure to read Installing a Channel Back, Page 73, before continuing.

▶ **Installing Seat Cover**

Before the seat cover can be installed, a 1/2-inch layer of cotton padding must be installed on the muslin. Go to Page 46 to install cotton padding.

The seat is the first section of the top cover to be installed. The seat may consist of a one piece seat cover, or a seat cover with a box strip, and a band strip.

The piece that covers the padded portion of the seat is installed first. This may be a single piece or it may be a cover with a machine sewn box strip.

After this section is installed, the band strip is installed if needed.

If a seat cover has machine sewn seams, they should fit snug around the padding before the cover is tacked to the frame.

1. Center seat cover [1] over seat. Arrange cover until any seams fit snugly over padding.

When tacking the cover to the frame, be sure to tack the cover to the rails recorded when the strip

was removed. Be sure to drive the number of tacks recorded when the cover was removed. Drive the tacks at the distances recorded when the tacks were removed.

A slip tack is a tack that is driven 1/2 its length into the frame.

2. Using tack hammer, drive one slip tack [2] through cover [1] into center of front rail [3].

Installing Seat Cover

3. Pull cover [2] tightly to one corner. Drive required slip tacks [1] through cover into rail [4].

4. Pull cover [2] tightly to opposite corner. Drive required slip tacks [3] through cover into rail [4].

When pulling cover to back rail, pull cover tightly, but not tight enough to compress springs and padding.

The cover may have to be pulled through the slot where the back and seat meet.

5. Pull cover [2] tightly to back rail.

Repeat Steps 2 through 4 to tack cover to back rail.

Installing Seat Cover

After the front and back edges of the seat cover are tacked to the frame, the sides must be tacked to the frame.

If the seat has an obstruction [2] that prevents the cover from being tacked to the side rails, the cover must be cut and fitted around the obstruction.

If the seat does not have an obstruction, go to Page 54.

6. Fold edge [1] of cover over until it just touches the obstruction [2].

When making the cut from the edge of the material to the obstruction, make the cut to within about 1/2-inch from the back edge [3] of the obstruction [2]. Any excess material left after cutting can be tucked between the back edge of the obstruction and the padding.

7. Using scissors, make a straight cut from edge of cover to obstruction.

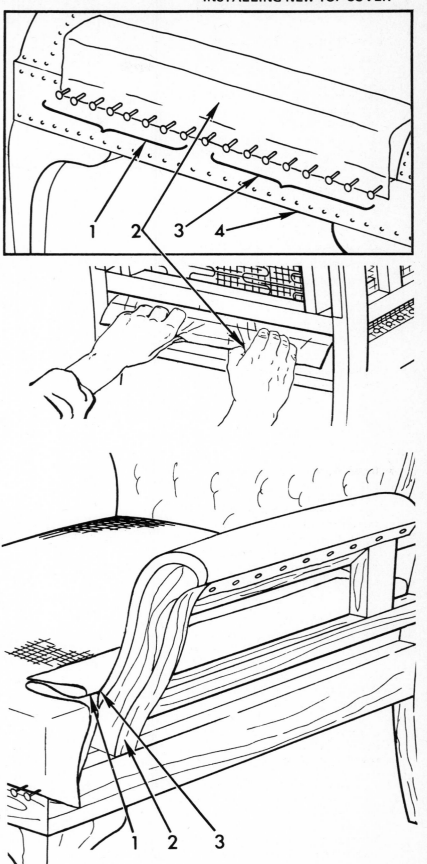

INSTALLING NEW TOP COVER

Installing Seat Cover

Excess material may have to be cut from the seat cover so that a neat edge can be formed along the sides of the obstruction [3].

Do this by making a diagonal cut at a slight angle to the straight cut. The cut must end near the edge of the obstruction.

8. Using scissors, make cut [1] at an angle to the first cut [2].

Any excess material remaining after the two cuts can be tucked between the padding and the obstruction.

If the excess material cannot be easily forced between the padding and obstruction, use a ruler to force the material into position or remove more material, if required.

9. Tuck excess material between padding and obstruction.

Installing Seat Cover

10. Pull edge of cover [4] to side rail [6]. Drive one slip tack [2] through cover between obstruction [3] and front corner.

11. Pull cover tightly to front corner. Drive required slip tacks [1] through cover into rail.

12. Pull cover tightly to obstruction [7]. Drive required slip tacks [5] through cover into rail.

13. Pull edge of cover to opposite side rail.

Repeat Steps 6 through 12 and tack edge of cover to side rail. Then go to Page 55.

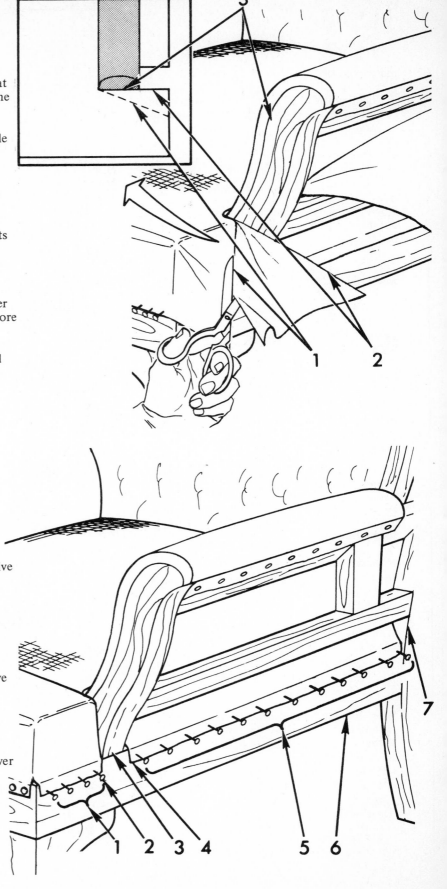

Installing Seat Cover

14. Pull cover to one side rail [2]. Drive one slip tack [3] through cover into center of side rail.

15. Pull cover tightly to front corner. Drive required slip tacks [1] through cover into rail [2].

16. Pull cover tightly to back corner. Drive required slip tacks [4] through cover into rail [2].

17. Pull cover tightly to opposite side rail. Drive one slip tack through cover into center of side rail.

Repeat Steps 15 and 16 to tack cover to side rail. Then go to section below.

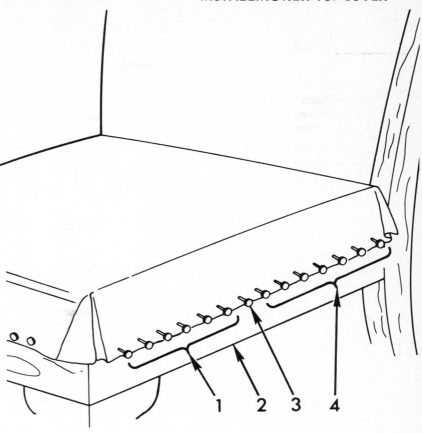

Installing Seat Cover

The seat cover is now tacked to the frame on all sides and fitted around any obstructions at the side.

The corners of the cover must now be fitted to insure that the cover fits the seat smoothly and evenly.

If the cover must fit around the back post, the cover will have to be cut to fit around the posts.

18. Using scissors, cut back corners of cover [2] to fit around back post [1].

If the old cover was pleated at the front corners, the new cover will have to be pleated at the corners.

19. Pleat front corners of cover. Drive one slip tack through pleat [3].

The cover is now cut, fitted, and slip tacked to the frame.

Carefully check that the seat is smooth and even. Be sure all edges and corners fit correctly. Be sure that the 1/2-inch layer of padding is smooth and even.

If the cover is not correctly installed, remove necessary slip tacks and readjust cover.

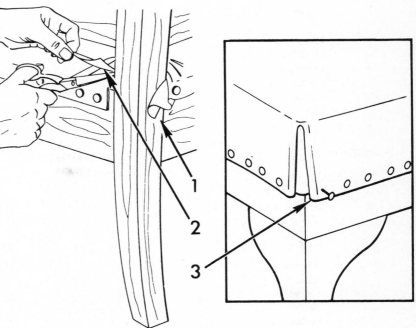

After the cover is correctly adjusted the tacks can be driven completely into the frame.

20. Drive all tacks completely into frame.

INSTALLING NEW TOP COVER

Installing Seat Cover

If the seat has a band strip, it must now be installed.

The band strip is blind tacked at the top edge and tacked at the bottom edge.

A welting strip is usually tacked between the band strip and the seat cover.

Before beginning to install the welting strip, read Installing Welting Strips, Page 51.

20. Install welting strip [1] to rail [2] at recorded position.

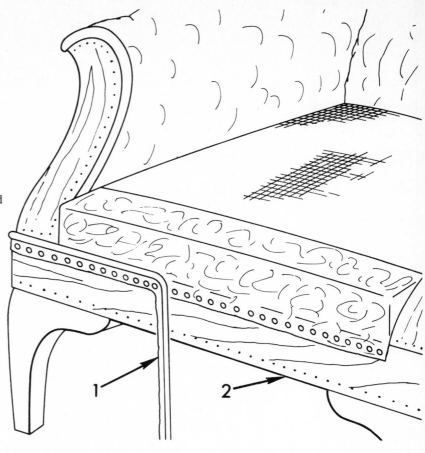

Installing Seat Cover

If the seat has a band strip, it must now be tacked to the frame.

The top edge is blind tacked to the frame to cover the raw edge of the seat cover and to cover the tacks holding the seat cover to the frame.

Before blind tacking the band strip to the frame, read Blind Tacking, Page 50.

21. Blind tack top edge of band strip [2] to rail [3].

22. Pull band strip [2] right side up over cardboard strip [1]. Pull cover tightly to bottom of rail [3]. Drive required tacks [4] through strip into rail.

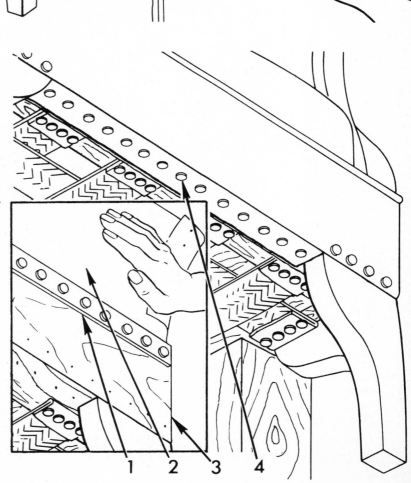

► **Installing Inside Wing Cover**

When installing the inside wing cover to the frame, be careful not to move or rearrange the padding.

The inside wing cover is tacked to the frame at all four rails.

1.   Center inside wing cover on wing frame.

When tacking the cover to the frame be sure to tack the cover to the rails recorded when the cover was removed. Be sure to drive the number of tacks recorded when the cover was removed. Drive the tacks at the distance recorded when the cover was removed.

2.   Using tack hammer, drive one slip tack [3] through cover into center of top wing rail [1].

3.   Pull cover tightly to front corner. Drive required slip tacks [4] through cover into rail.

4.   Pull cover tightly to back corner. Drive required slip tacks [2] through cover into rail.

When pulling cover to arm board [5], pull cover tightly, but not tight enough to compress padding.

5.   Pull cover tightly to arm board [5].

Repeat Steps 2 through 4 to slip tack cover to arm board.

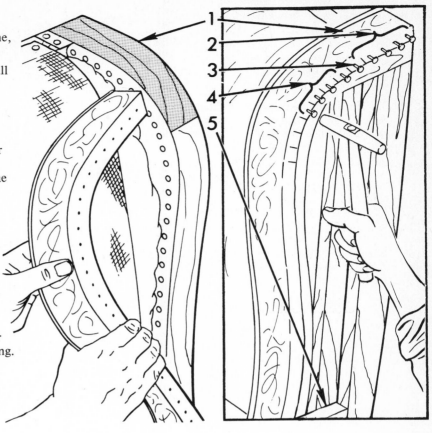

Installing Inside Wing Cover

The inside wing cover may have to be pleated to fit the contour of the wing post.

6.   Pull cover tightly to wing post [1].

7.   Drive one slip tack [4] through cover into center of post [1].

8.   Pull cover tightly to top corner. Drive required slip tacks [3] through cover into post.

9.   Pull cover tightly to bottom corner. Drive required slip tacks [5] through cover into post.

The cover may have to be pulled through the slot where the wing and the seat meet.

10.   Pull cover tightly to back post [2].

Repeat Steps 7 through 9 to slip tack cover to back post.

Carefully check that the wing is smooth and even. Be sure all edges and corners fit correctly. Be sure that the 1/2-inch layer of padding is smooth and even.

If the cover is not correctly installed, remove necessary slip tacks and adjust cover.

After the cover is correctly adjusted, the tacks must be driven completely into the frame.

11.   Drive all tacks completely into frame.

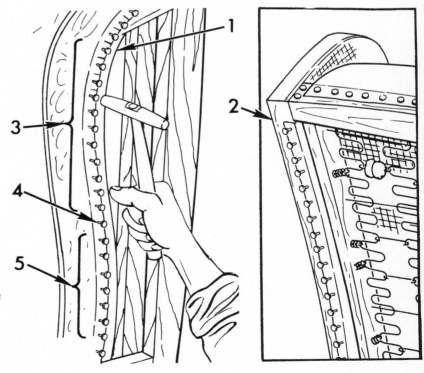

INSTALLING NEW TOP COVER

▶ **Installing Inside Arm Cover**

Before the inside arm cover can be installed, a 1/2-inch layer of cotton must be installed on the muslin. Go to Page 46 to install cotton padding.

The inside arm cover is usually tacked to the frame on all four sides. If installing cover to a wing back chair, the part of the inside arm cover that meets the inside wing cover must be blind stitched to the inside wing cover.

1. Center inside arm cover over arm.

When tacking the cover to the frame, be sure to tack the cover to the rails recorded when the strip was removed. Be sure to drive the number of tacks recorded when the cover was removed. Drive the tacks at the distances recorded when the cover was removed.

2. Using tack hammer, drive one slip tack [2] through cover into center of arm board [3].

3. Pull cover tightly to front corner. Drive required slip tacks [1] through cover into rail.

4. Pull cover tightly to back corner. Drive required slip tacks [4] through cover into rail.

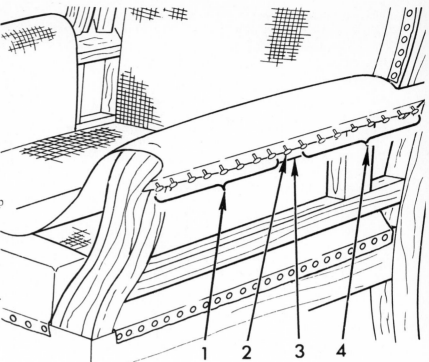

Installing Inside Arm Cover

If the inside arm cover must be blind stitched to the inside wing cover, be sure to read Blind Stitching, Page 50, before continuing.

5. Blind stitch inside arm cover to inside wing cover.

When pulling cover to bottom rail, pull cover tightly but not tight enough to compress padding.

The cover may have to be pulled through the slot where the arm and seat meet.

6. Pull cover tightly to bottom rail [1].

Repeat Steps 2 through 4 to tack cover to bottom rail.

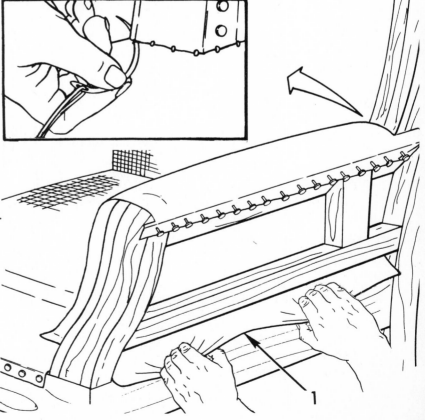

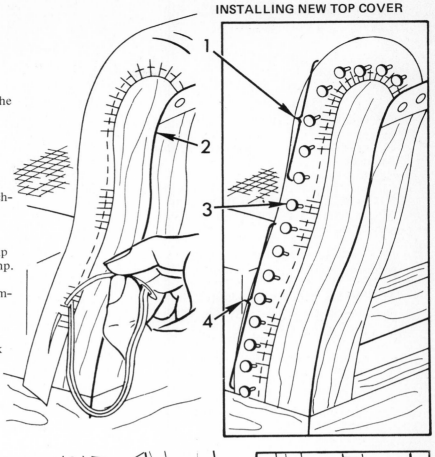

Installing Inside Arm Cover

The front edge of the cover must be tacked to the arm stump [2].

If the stump is rounded, the cover must be gathered and stitched to fit the shape of the arm stump.

6. Using curved upholsterer's needle and stitching twine, gather and stitch front edge of cover to fit shape of arm stump.

7. Pull cover to arm stump [2]. Drive one slip tack [3] through cover into center of stump.

8. Pull cover to top of stump. Using tack hammer, drive required slip tacks [1] through cover into stump.

9. Pull cover to bottom of stump. Using tack hammer, drive required slip tacks [4] through cover into stump.

Installing Inside Arm Cover

The cover may have to be pulled through the slot where the back and arm meet.

The cover must be tacked to the back post [1] or the arm slat [2] as recorded when cover was removed.

10. Pull cover tightly to back post [1] or arm slat [2]. Drive one slip tack through cover into center of post or slat.

Repeat Steps 8 and 9 to tack cover to back post or arm slat.

If the cover does not fit correctly around back posts, the cover must be cut to fit exactly around the posts.

11. Using scissors, cut corners to fit around back post [1].

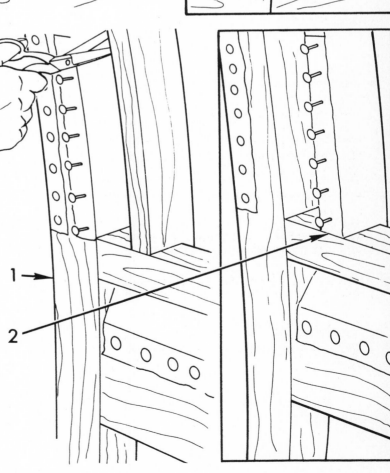

INSTALLING NEW TOP COVER

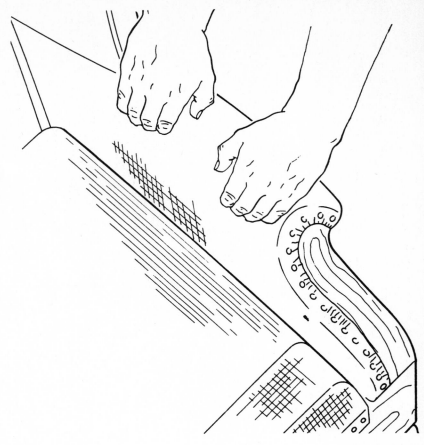

Installing Inside Arm Cover

The cover is now cut, fitted, and slip tacked to the frame.

Carefully check that the seat is smooth and even. Be sure all edges and corners fit correctly. Be sure that the 1/2-inch layer of padding is smooth and even.

If the cover is not correctly installed, remove necessary slip tacks and adjust cover.

After the cover is correctly adjusted, the tacks must be driven completely into the frame.

12. Drive all tacks completely into frame.

▶ **Installing Inside Back Cover**

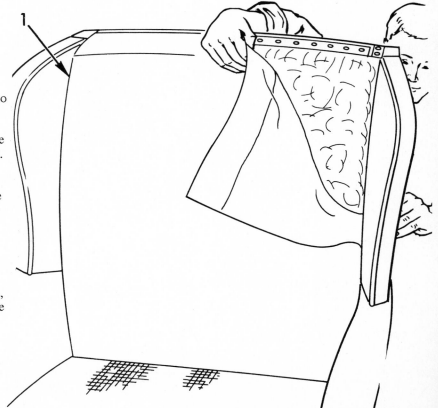

Before the inside back cover can be installed, a 1/2-inch layer of cotton padding must be installed over the muslin cover. Go to Page 46 to install cotton padding.

The inside back cover may consist of a one-piece cover, or a cover with a box strip and band strip.

The piece that covers the padded portion of the back is installed first. This may be a single piece or it may be a cover with a machine sewn box strip.

After this is installed the band strip is installed, if needed.

If the inside back cover has machine sewn seams, they should fit snugly around the padding before the cover is tacked to the frame.

1. Center inside back cover [1] over back. Arrange cover until any seams fit snugly over padding.

Installing Inside Back Cover

A slip tack is a tack that is driven 1/2 its length into the frame.

When tacking the cover to the frame, be sure to tack the cover to the rails recorded when the cover was removed. Be sure to drive the number of tacks recorded when the cover was removed. Be sure to drive the tacks at the distances recorded when the cover was removed.

2.   Using tack hammer, drive one slip tack [2] through cover into top rail [4].

3.   Pull cover tightly to one corner. Drive required slip tacks [1] through cover into top rail.

4.   Pull cover tightly to opposite corner. Drive required slip tacks [3] through cover into top rail.

When pulling cover to bottom rail [5], pull the cover tightly but not tight enough to compress springs and padding.

The cover may have to be pulled through the slot where the back and seat meet.

5.   Pull cover tightly to bottom rail [5].

Repeat Steps 2 through 4 to tack cover to bottom rail.

Installing Inside Back Cover

The cover must now be tacked to the side rails.

6.   Pull cover to one side rail [1]. Drive one slip tack [3] through cover into center of side rail.

7.   Pull cover tightly to top corner. Drive required slip tacks [2] through cover into rail.

8.   Pull cover to bottom corner. Drive required slip tacks [4] through cover into rail.

9.   Pull cover to opposite side rail. Drive one slip tack through cover into center of rail.

Repeat Steps 7 and 8 to tack cover to side rail.

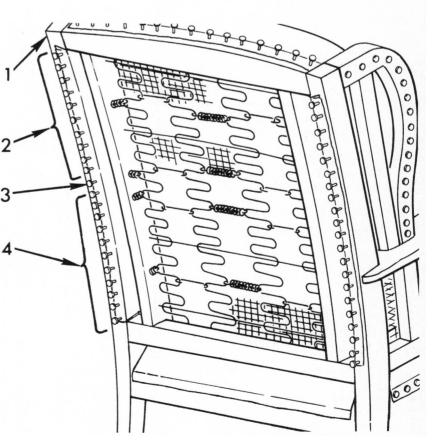

INSTALLING NEW TOP COVER

Installing Inside Back Cover

The back cover is now tacked to the frame on all sides.

The corners of the cover may have to be fitted to insure that the cover fits the back smoothly and evenly.

If the cover must fit around the arm board the cover will have to be cut and fitted around the arm board.

10. Using scissors, cut cover to fit around arm board [1].

If the old cover was pleated at the top corners, the new cover will have to be pleated at the corners.

11. Pleat corners [2]. Drive one slip tack through pleat.

The cover is now cut, fitted, and slip tacked to the frame.

Carefully check that the back cover is smooth and even. Be sure all edges and corners fit correctly. Be sure that the 1/2-inch layer of padding is smooth and even.

If the cover is not correctly installed, remove necessary slip tacks and adjust the cover.

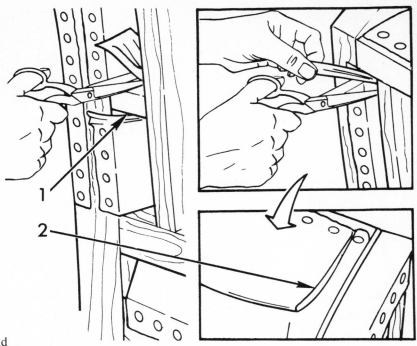

After the cover is correctly adjusted, the slip tacks must be driven completely into the rail.

12. Drive all tacks completely into frame.

Installing Inside Back Cover

If the back has a band strip, it must now be installed.

The band strip is blind tacked at the front edge and tacked at the back and side edges.

A welting strip is usually tacked between the installed back cover and the band strip.

Before beginning to install the welting strip be sure to read Installing Welting Strips, Page 51.

Be sure that welting strip is installed at position recorded when strip was removed.

13. Install welting strip [1] at recorded position.

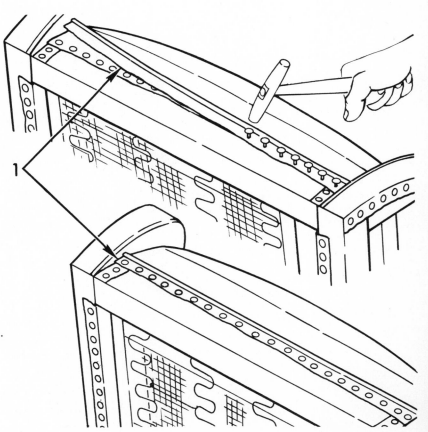

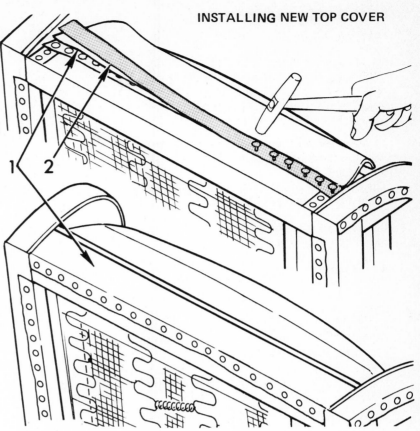

Installing Inside Back Cover

After welting strips are installed, the band strip [1] can be installed.

The front edge of the band strip [1] is blind tacked to the frame to cover the raw edge of the back cover and to cover the tacks holding the cover or welting strip to the frame.

Before blind tacking the band strip to the frame read Blind Tacking, Page 50.

14.　Blind tack front edge of band strip [1] to frame.

15.　Pull cover right side out over cardboard strip [2]. Pull cover tightly to back rail. Drive required tacks through cover into rail.

▶ **Installing Outside Wing Cover**

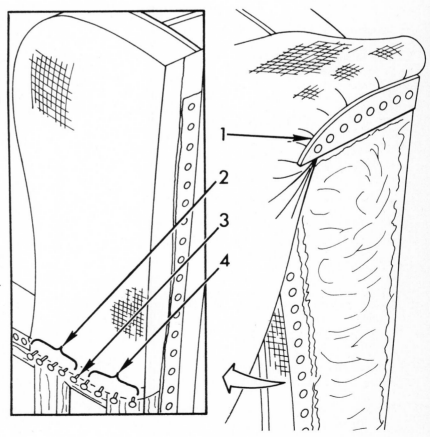

The outside wing cover is blind tacked to the frame at the top, tacked at the bottom and back edge, and blind stitched at the front edge.

Before blind tacking the outside wing cover to the frame, read Blind Tacking, Page 50.

1.　Blind tack top edge of outside arm cover to wing rail [1].

When tacking the cover to the frame, be sure to tack the cover to the rails recorded when the cover was removed. Be sure to drive the number of tacks recorded when the cover was removed. Be sure to drive the tacks at the distances recorded when the cover was removed.

2.　Pull cover right side out over cardboard strip. Pull cover to arm board. Drive one slip tack [3] through cover into center of arm board.

3.　Pull cover to front corner. Drive required slip tacks [2] through cover into arm board.

4.　Pull cover to back corner. Drive required slip tacks [4] through cover into arm board.

INSTALLING NEW TOP COVER

Installing Outside Wing Cover

5.   Pull cover to back post [1]. Drive one slip tack [3] through cover into center of post.

6.   Pull cover to top corner. Drive required slip tacks [2] through cover into post.

7.   Pull cover to bottom corner. Drive required slip tacks [4] through cover into post.

The front edge of the cover must be blind stitched to the inside wing cover.

Before blind stitching cover to inside arm cover read Blind Stitching, Page 50.

8.   Blind stitch front edge of cover to inside arm cover.

Carefully check that the outside wing cover is smooth and even. Be sure all edges and corners fit correctly. Be sure that the 1/2-inch layer of padding is smooth and even.

If the cover is not correctly installed, remove necessary slip tacks and adjust cover.

After the cover is correctly adjusted the tacks must be driven completely into the frame.

9.   Drive all tacks completely into frame.

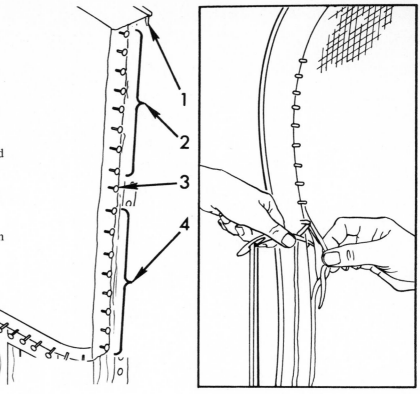

▶ **Installing Outside Arm Cover**

The outside arm cover is installed after all the padded sections of the chair are covered.

The outside arm cover covers all the interior components of the arm and covers the tacks holding the inside arm cover to the frame.

The outside arm cover may be installed to the frame by one or more of the following methods as recorded when disassembled:

● Decorative tacks at top and sides

● Tacks covered with gimp at top and sides

● Tacks at front and back

● Blind tacks at top

● Blind stitches at front

If cover is installed with decorative tacks or staples covered with gimp, go to Page 66.

If cover is blind tacked at top, continue.

Before blind tacking the outside arm cover to the frame, read Blind Tacking, Page 50.

1.   Blind tack top edge of outside arm cover to arm board [1].

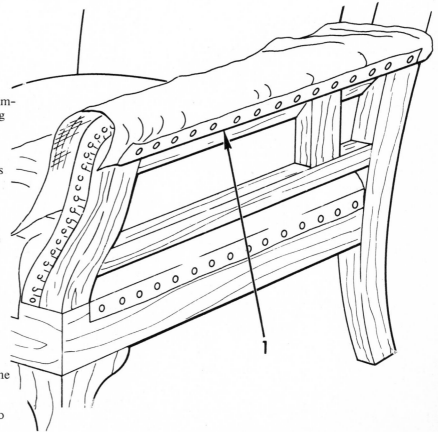

Installing Outside Arm Cover

2. Pull cover right side out over cardboard strip. Pull cover tightly to bottom rail [2]. Using tack hammer, drive one slip tack [3] through cover into center of rail.

3. Pull cover to front corner. Drive required slip tacks [1] through cover into rail.

4. Pull cover to back corner. Drive required slip tacks [4] through cover into rail.

5. Pull cover to back post [5]. Drive one slip tack [7] through cover into center of post.

6. Pull cover to top corner. Drive required slip tacks [6] through cover into post.

7. Pull cover to bottom corner. Drive required slip tacks [8] through cover into post.

If cover is installed with decorative tacks or staples covered with gimp, go to Page 66.

If the front of the chair arm is covered with a panel, the cover is tacked to the arm stump. Continue.

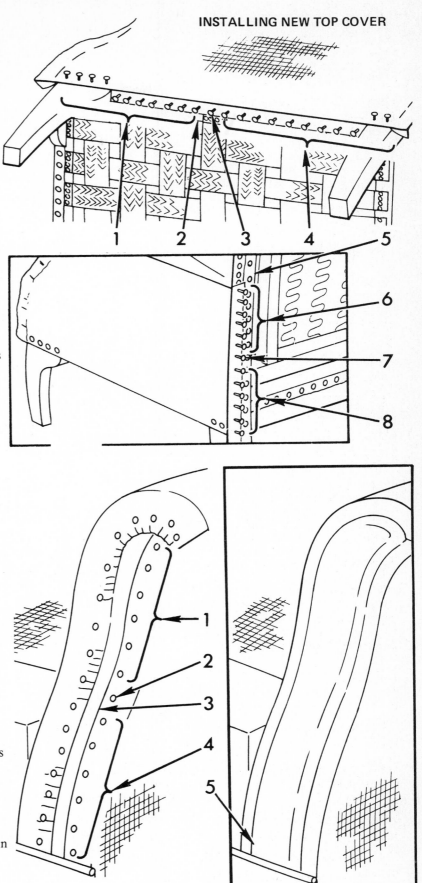

Installing Outside Arm Cover

8. Pull cover to arm stump [3]. Drive one slip tack [2] through cover to center of stump.

9. Pull cover to top corner. Drive required slip tacks [1] through cover into stump.

10. Pull cover to bottom corner. Drive required slip tacks [4] through cover into stump.

The cover is now cut, fitted, and slip tacked to the frame.

Carefully check that outside arm cover is smooth and even. Be sure all edges and corners fit correctly.

If the cover is not correctly installed, remove necessary slip tacks and adjust cover.

After the cover is correctly adjusted, the slip tacks must be driven completely into the rails.

11. Using tack hammer, drive all tacks completely into rails.

The front panel [5] must now be installed. Install the panel in the same way as recorded when the original panel was removed.

12. Install front panel [5].

INSTALLING NEW TOP COVER

Installing Outside Arm Cover

Before blind stitching the outside arm cover [1] to the inside arm cover [2], read Blind Stitching, Page 50.

13.   Fold raw edge of outside cover under cover [1]. Align folded edge with inside arm cover [2] or welting strip.

14.   While holding folded edge at aligned position, pin edge to inside arm cover.

15.   Blind stitch cover to inside arm cover.

Carefully check that outside arm cover is smooth and even. Be sure all corners fit correctly.

If the cover is not correctly installed remove necessary slip tacks and adjust cover.

After the cover is correctly adjusted, the slip tacks must be driven completely into the rails.

16.   Drive all slip tacks completely into rails.

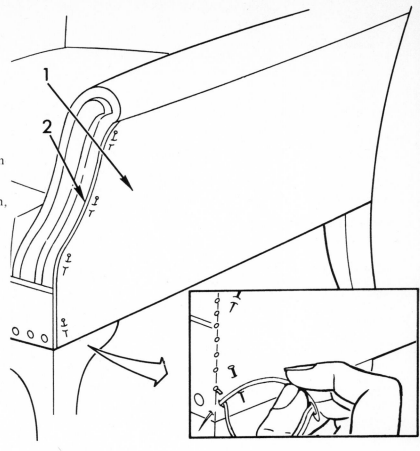

Installing Outside Arm Cover

If the old cover was installed with staples, use tacks instead of staples when installing new cover.

All decorative tacks and tacks to be covered with gimp are installed in the same manner.

Begin with the top edge. Next, do the bottom edge. Then do the two side edges.

17.   Fold raw edge of outside arm cover [4] under approximately 1/2-inch. Align folded edge with welting strip or inside arm cover.

18.   Drive one slip tack [2] through cover into center of rail.

19.   Pull cover tightly to one corner. Drive required slip tacks [3] through cover into rail.

20.   Pull cover tightly to opposite corner. Drive required slip tacks [1] through cover into rail.

21.   Pull cover to opposite rail [5]. Repeat Steps 17 through 20.

Repeat Steps 17 through 21 until all sides are slip tacked to the rails.

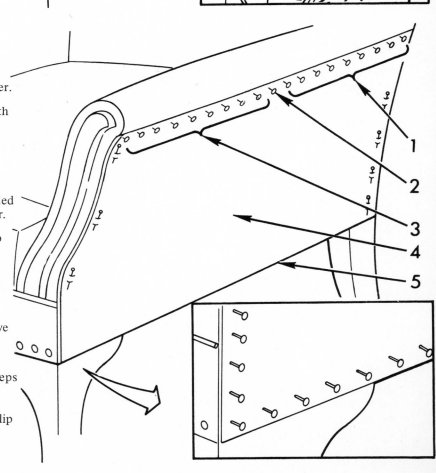

Installing Outside Arm Cover

Carefully check that cover is smooth and even. Be sure all edges and corners fit correctly.

If the cover is not installed correctly, remove necessary slip tacks and adjust the corner.

After the cover is correctly adjusted, the slip tacks must be driven completely into the rail.

22.   Drive all slip tacks completely into rails.

Install the gimp [1] over each exposed tack at the locations recorded when the tacks were removed.

23.   Using white glue, install gimp [1].

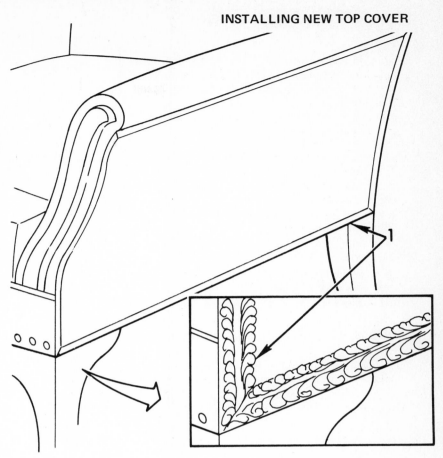

▶ **Installing Outside Back Cover**

The outside back cover is the last section of the top cover to be installed.

The outside back cover covers all the interior components of the back and covers the tacks holding the inside arm cover and outside wing cover to the frame.

The outside back cover may be installed to the frame by one or more of the following methods as recorded when disassembled:

- Decorative tacks
- Tacks covered with gimp
- Blind tacks at top
- Blind stitches at sides
- Tacks at bottom

If cover is installed with decorative tacks or staples covered with gimp, go to Page 68.

If cover is blind tacked at the top, continue.

Before blind tacking the outside back cover to the frame, read Blind Tacking, Page 50.

1.   Blind tack top edge of outside back cover to top back rail [1].

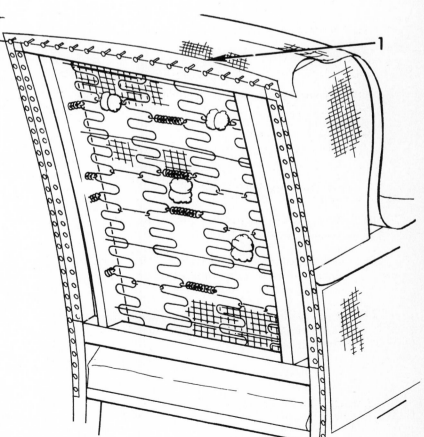

INSTALLING NEW TOP COVER

Installing Outside Back Cover

2. Pull cover over cardboard strip. Pull cover to bottom rail [1]. Using tack hammer, drive one slip tack [3] through cover into center of rail.

3. Pull cover to one side corner. Using tack hammer, drive required slip tacks [2] through cover into rail.

4. Pull cover to opposite side corner. Using tack hammer, drive required slip tacks [4] through cover into rail.

Before beginning to blind stitch the outside back cover to the inside back cover, be sure to read Blind Stitching, Page 50.

5. Fold raw edge of one side under. Align edge with inside arm cover or welting strip.

6. While holding folded edge at aligned position, pin edge to inside back cover [5].

7. Blind stitch one side to inside back cover [5] and inside arm cover.

Repeat Steps 5 through 7 for opposite side of cover.

Carefully check that outside back cover is smooth and even. Be sure all corners fit correctly.

If the cover is not correctly installed, remove necessary slip tacks and adjust cover.

After the cover is correctly adjusted, the slip tacks must be driven completely into the rails.

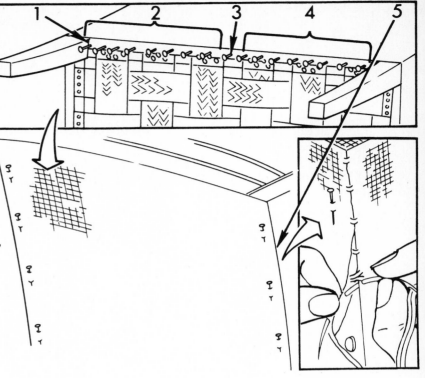

8. Using tack hammer, drive all slip tacks completely into rails.

Installing Outside Back Cover

All decorative tacks and tacks to be covered with gimp are installed in the same manner.

Begin with the top edge. Next, do the bottom edge. Then do the two side edges.

9. Fold raw edge of cover under approximately 1/2-inch. Align folded edge with welting strip or inside back cover.

10. Using tack hammer, drive one slip tack [2] through cover into rail [4].

11. Pull cover tightly to one corner. Using tack hammer drive required slip tacks [1] through cover into rail.

12. Pull cover tightly to opposite corner. Using tack hammer, drive required slip tacks [3] through cover into rail.

13. Pull cover to opposite rail [5] and repeat Steps 9 through 12.

Repeat Steps 9 through 13 until all sides are slip tacked to the rails.

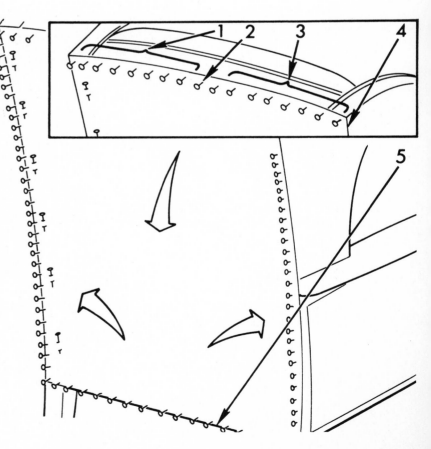

Installing Outside Back Cover

Carefully check that cover is smooth and even.
Be sure all edges and corners fit correctly.

If the cover is not installed correctly remove
necessary slip tacks and adjust the cover.

After the cover is correctly adjusted the slip tacks
must be driven completely into the rail.

14. Using tack hammer, drive all slip tacks
     completely into rails.

If gimp [1] must be installed, continue.

Install the gimp [1] over exposed tacks at the
locations recorded when the tacks were
removed.

15. Using white glue, install gimp [1].

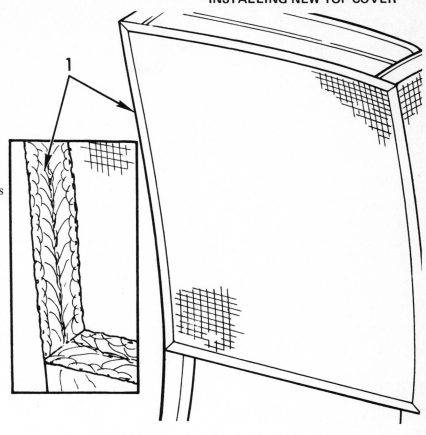

▶ **Installing Skirt**

If the chair has a skirt [1], it is the last top cover
section to be installed.

The skirt is blind tacked at the top edge and free
at the bottom edge.

A welting strip [2] is usually sewn onto top of
the skirt [1]. Then the skirt with welting strip
attached is blind tacked to the frame. Instructions for sewing a welting strip are on Page 49.

1. Sew welting strip [2]. Sew welting strip
    to top of skirt [1].

Before blind tacking the skirt to the frame, read
Blind Tacking, Page 50.

2. Blind tack top edge of skirt [1] to frame.

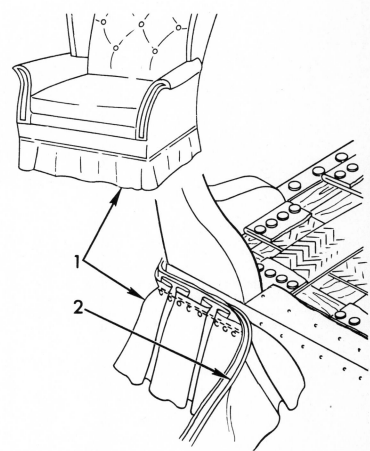

INSTALLING NEW TOP COVER

▶ **Installing Cambrick Dust Cover**

The cambrick dust cover is the last part of the chair to be installed.

If the old cambrick cover cannot be used, it should be used as a pattern to cut the new cover. Allow enough material for a fold [3] along the edges of the cover.

1. Using scissors, cut cambrick to size of old cover.

All edges of cover [2] should have a fold [3] to make a smooth outer edge. Tacks are installed through both layers of fold.

2. Place one edge of cover [2] on one bottom rail. Using tack hammer, drive one tack [1] through center of cover into rail.

3. Pull cover to one corner. Drive required slip tacks through cover into rail.

4. Pull cover to opposite corner. Drive required slip tacks through cover into rail.

5. Pull cover tightly to opposite rail. Drive one tack through center of cover into rail.

Repeat Steps 3 and 4 to tack edge to rail.

Repeat Steps 2 through 4 to tack remaining edges to rails.

▶ **Installing Tufted Back**

The tufted pattern is made by pulling buttons [1] deeply into the back cushion [2] and joining them with deep creases [3]. The diamond-shaped or square-shaped pattern resulting from these creases is determined by the locations of the buttons.

The buttons are held in their proper locations by tying them securely to a burlap back cover [4]. This burlap back cover is exposed when the top cover is removed from the back of the furniture item.

The old burlap back cover must be replaced with new burlap. However, because it provides the pattern for properly locating buttons, it must be retained for marking the new burlap.

If the back cushion material is damaged, it should be replaced. It is generally recommended that it be replaced with 4-inch thick polyurethane foam. The old burlap back cover is used as a pattern for marking button hole locations on the new foam cushion.

1. Using old burlap back cover [4] as a guide mark pattern on new burlap. Cut burlap to size.

2. Install new burlap back cover to frame.

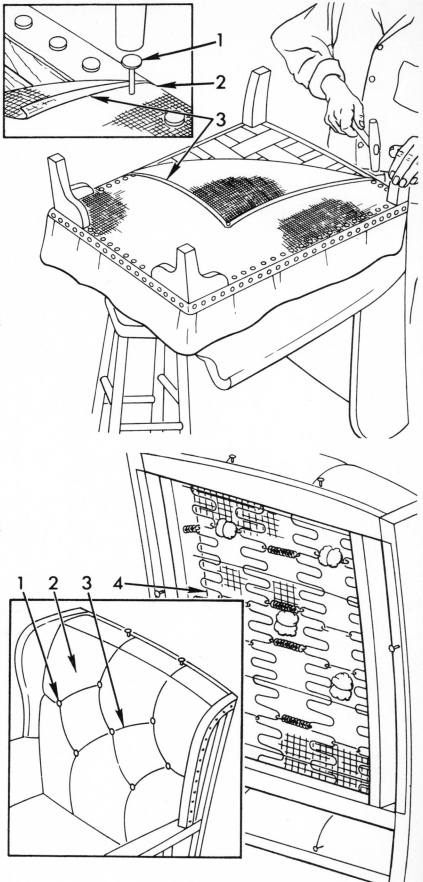

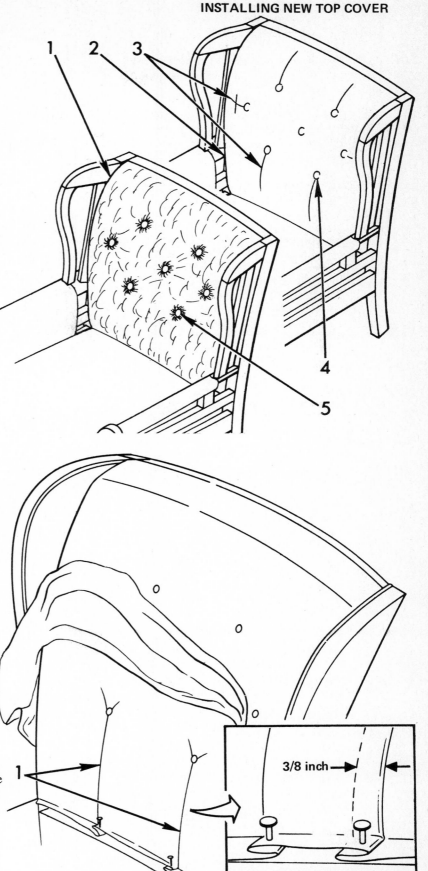

Installing Tufted Back

3. Using old burlap cover as a guide, mark pattern on foam [2].

At each place where a button is to be installed a hole [4] must be made through the foam.

4. Make hole [4] in foam [2] at location of each button.

If the cover has horizontal and vertical creases at the top bottom and sides, horizontal and vertical slits [3] must be cut in the foam at the location of the creases.

5. Cut horizontal and vertical slits [3] in foam.

6. Place 1/2-inch layer of cotton padding [1] over foam. Make hole [5] in cotton at location of each hole in foam.

7. Install foam [2] and cotton padding [1].

Installing Tufted Back

The old top cover must be pressed flat and all the pleats removed. The pattern left by the button holes on the old cover must be transferred to the new pattern.

8. Using old top cover as a guide, mark pattern of button holes on new top cover.

The top cover material must now be installed. Each pleat [1] must be formed at the bottom edge. The pleat is then tacked to the bottom rail.

Begin with the center pleat and work toward the edge pleats.

Each pleat is formed by folding 3/8-inch of material under. Each pleat must be formed with the marked line in the center of the inside fold.

9. Make pleat [1]. Place pleat on bottom rail so that it is even with cut in foam. Drive one slip tack through pleat. Be sure to drive tacks in correct side of rail as noted during disassembly.

Repeat Step 9 until all bottom vertical pleats are completed.

3/8 inch

INSTALLING NEW TOP COVER

Installing Tufted Back

The bottom row of buttons [1] must be installed. Begin with the center button and work to the edge buttons.

Use a straight upholsterer's needle and twine to install the button. The twine must be a double length. It must be long enough to pass through all the padding.

10. Thread button onto twine. Insert both ends of twine through eye of needle.

In next step, needle will pull both ends of twine completely through chair back. Button will be held in place by twine.

11. While holding twine through needle, push needle completely through chair back at location of hole in padding.

12. Form pleat [2] below button. Pull twine tightly, pulling button deeply into hole. Tie twine tightly. Place a small wad of cotton between knot and back.

Repeat Steps 10 through 12 until the bottom row of buttons is installed.

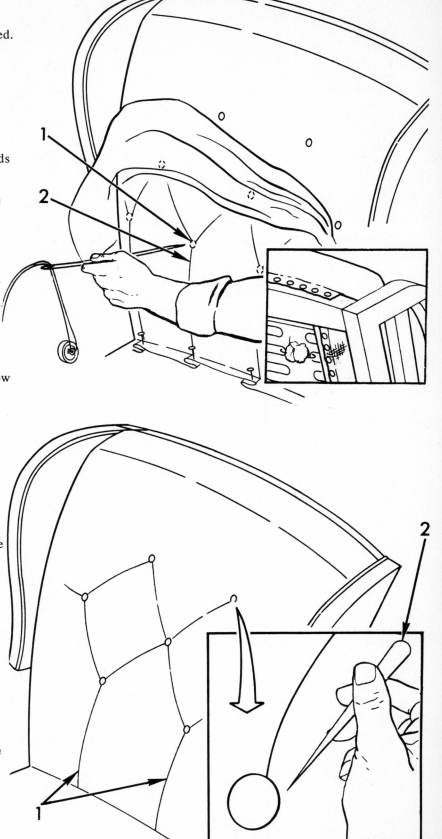

Installing Tufted Back

After all of the bottom buttons are installed, the pleats [1] must be made smooth and even. A stuffing regulator [2] is slipped into the pleat and pressed against the inner fold to make the pleat smooth and even.

13. Using stuffing regulator [2], adjust pleats.

As the remaining buttons are installed, the tufts will be formed. Install one horizontal row of buttons at a time.

As each button is installed, form the pleats necessary to form the tuft.

Repeat Steps 10 through 13 until all buttons are installed and all tufts are made.

Installing Tufted Back

The top vertical pleats [1] are made the same as the bottom vertical pleats [5]. Repeat Step 9 to complete all top vertical pleats. Read notes preceding Step 9.

If the chair has horizontal side pleats [4], they must be formed. These pleats are made the same way as the vertical pleats. Repeat Step 9 to complete the side horizontal pleats. Read notes preceding Step 9.

14.   Pull side of cover around back post [2]. Drive required slip tacks [3] into post.

Repeat Step 14 for remaining side.

The loose edges of the bottom and top must now be slip tacked to the frame.

15.   Drive required slip tacks to bottom frame [6]. Drive required slip tacks to top frame [7].

16.   Drive all slip tacks completely into the frame.

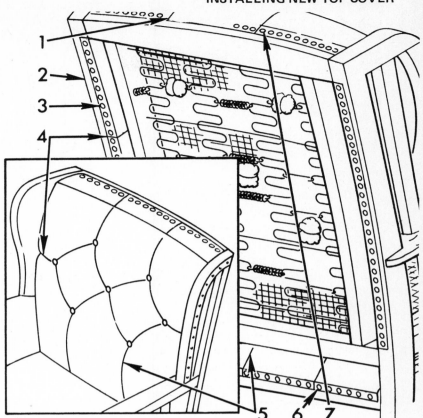

▶ **Installing Channeled Back**

A channeled back [2] is sewn and stuffed before being installed. Then it is installed to the back in the same way as a plain back cover.

The outer half of the channeled cover is made from the top cover material and the inner half is made from muslin. A piece of muslin is used at the bottom as a stretcher.

A stretcher is a piece of inexpensive material sewn to the bottom and used to hold the cover to the back frame.

The channels will vary according to the type of chair you have. For straight back chairs, the channels are the same width at the top and bottom. For curved back or shell back chairs, the top of each channel is wider than the bottom.

The old top cover must be separated from its muslin cover and stretcher before it can be used as a pattern.

1.   Using scissors, cut and remove stitches [3] holding stretcher [4] to back cover. Remove all padding.

2.   Using scissors, cut all stitches [1] forming channels.

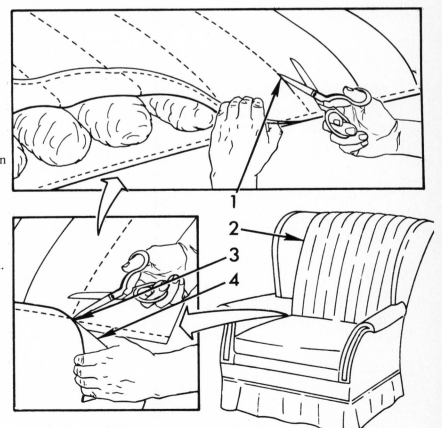

INSTALLING NEW TOP COVER

Installing Channeled Back

The separate sections must be pressed before they can be used as a pattern.

3. Using iron, press material until it is smooth and flat.

4. Using old back section as a pattern, cut muslin to correct size.

5. Using old stretcher as a pattern, cut muslin to correct size.

6. Using old top cover as a pattern, cut new top cover to correct size.

After the pieces are cut to size, they must be marked with the pattern of the channels.
The pattern can be seen where the old seams were cut and removed.

7. Using old back section as a guide, transfer pattern to new muslin.

8. Using old top cover as a guide, transfer pattern to back side of new cover material.

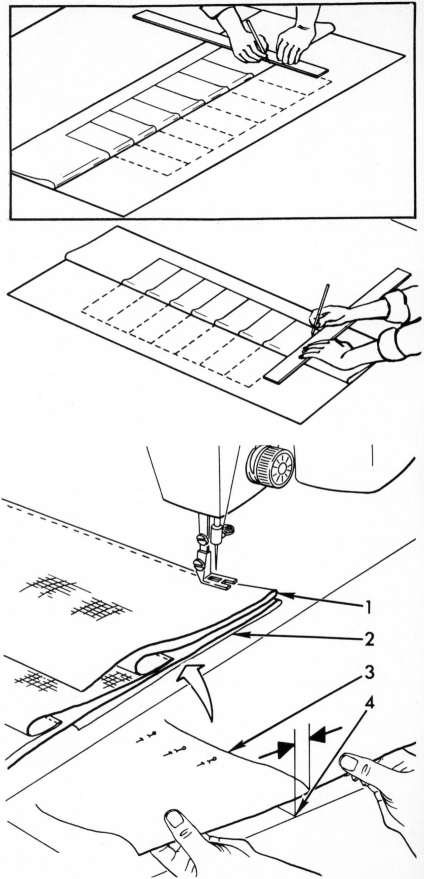

Installing Channeled Back

When sewing, sew channels only as near the top and bottom edges as the old material was sewn. Excess material must be left at the bottom to sew the stretcher material.

Begin at one side and work to the opposite side.

9. Place top cover material [1] over muslin [2]. Place line [3] on top cover material approximately 1/4-inch from line [4] on muslin. Pin material.

When sewing, fold the material back and sew down the middle of the tuck.

10. Machine sew seam.

Repeat Steps 9 and 10 until all channels are sewn.

After all channels are sewn, they must be stuffed with padding.

Installing Channeled Back

The padding may be foam or cotton. Use the old padding to determine the width, length, and thickness of padding.

11. Cut padding to correct size.

Two yardsticks should be used to force stuffing into the channels. Be sure to leave approximately 3 inches at end of yardsticks for tying the sticks together.

If the channeling is wider at the top than at the bottom, be sure that the bottom end of the padding is near the end of the sticks.

12. Place padding [2] between two yard-sticks [3]. Tie sticks together at the end.

13. Force yardsticks into channel [1] until padding is in correct position.

14. Untie sticks. Pull out top stick without disturbing padding. Pull out bottom stick without disturbing padding.

Repeat Steps 11 through 14 until all channels are stuffed.

15. Machine sew stretcher to bottom of cover.

Cover may now be installed. Go to Page 60 to install cover.

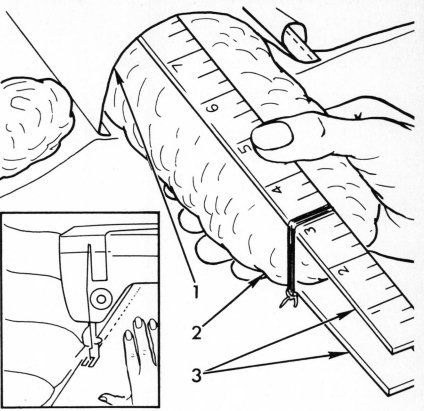

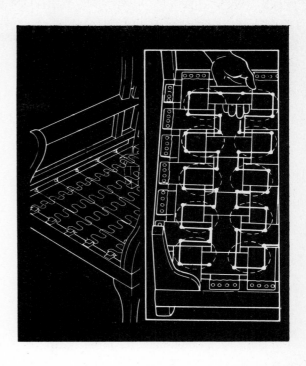

MINOR REPAIRS

▶ **Preparation**

If a chair has a sagging seat, but is in otherwise good condition, the seat may sometimes be repaired without disassembling the chair.

When a seat sags, the webbing bands, springs, or padding may be in need of repair. However, only the webbing bands can be repaired without disassembling the chair.

Sagless spring seats have no webbing bands supporting the springs. If a sagless spring chair should sag, it must be disassembled to be repaired.

To determine if the springs or padding are the problem, sit in the seat. If it has lumps or bulges, the springs or padding must be repaired or replaced.

If the seat sags, but has no lumps or bulges, the webbing bands are usually the problem.

There are three methods available for repairing a sagging seat without having to take the chair apart:

● Restretching Existing Webbing Bands
● Rewebbing With New Jute Webbing Bands
● Reinforcing With Steel Webbing Bands

The method to be used depends upon the condition of the existing bands.

Restretching existing bands is not difficult, but can only be done if the existing bands are in good condition.

For badly deteriorating bands, new jute webbing bands or steel webbing bands must be installed. Both are effective repairs, but reinforcing with steel webbing bands is the simpler.

A sagging seat can also be raised by reinforcing with a plywood board. To do this, cut a piece of plywood board to size of the chair bottom. Attach the board to the rails with wood screws.

This method is not recommended because it makes the seat hard and uncomfortable, and the exposed edges of the plywood board present an unsightly appearance.

To repair a sagging seat, do the following:

● Remove the cambrick dust cover.
● Inspect the seat from the bottom and determine which repair to perform.
● Make the repair.
● Install the cambrick dust cover.

▶ **Tools and Supplies**

The following tools and supplies may be required to repair a sagging seat:

● Hammer [1] and common screwdriver [2] for removing tacks from the frame.
● Scissors [3] for cutting twine holding springs to webbing bands.
● Self-locking pliers [4] for restretching existing webbing or stretching steel webbing bands.
● Magnetic tack hammer [5] for driving tacks into the frame.
● Jute webbing stretcher [6] for stretching new jute webbing bands.
● Steel webbing stretcher [7] for stretching steel webbing bands.
● Triangle file [8] for removing excess ends from steel webbing bands.
● Jute webbing [9] if installing new jute webbing bands.
● Corrugated steel webbing bands [10] or perforated steel webbing bands [11] if reinforcing with steel webbing bands.

● Twine for tying springs when installing new jute webbing.
● 12 ounce or 14 ounce upholstery tacks.

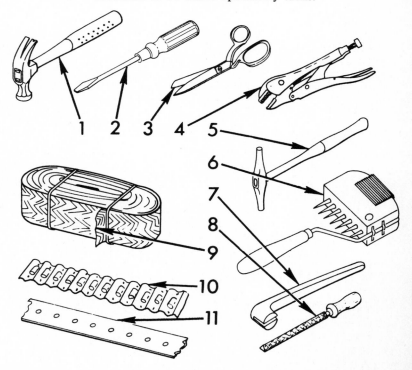

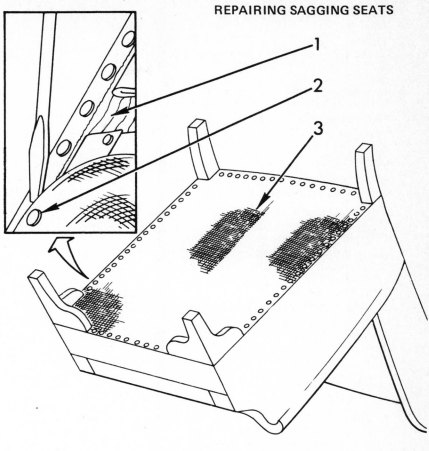

▶ Removing Cambrick Dust Cover

A cambrick dust cover [3] is a panel of stiff, coarse, black material. It is fastened to the bottom of the seat with tacks [2]. It must be removed to examine the bottom of the seat.

A tack is removed by forcing the blade of a common screwdriver under the tack head and prying the tack from the wood.

When removing a tack, always force the tack in the same direction as the wood grain [1]. By forcing the tack across the wood grain, you could split the wood.

1. Using hammer and screwdriver, remove all tacks [2] holding dust cover [3] to frame. Remove dust cover.

▶ Inspecting Seat

The interior of the seat must be inspected to determine if the seat can be repaired without disassembly and which repair should be attempted.

When looking into the bottom of the chair, you will see either sagless springs [2] or webbing bands [1].

If the chair has sagless springs, it must be disassembled to be repaired.

If the chair has webbing bands [1], it may be repaired without disassembling.

1. Check that bands [1] are not worn, torn, or deteriorating.

If the bands [1] are not worn, torn, or deteriorating, they can be restretched. Go to Page 80 to restretch existing bands.

If the bands are worn, torn, or deteriorating, they cannot be restretched. The seat must be rewebbed with new jute webbing bands or reinforced with steel webbing bands.

Read Rewebbing With New Jute Webbing Bands, Page 81, and Reinforcing With Steel Webbing Bands, Page 83, to determine which method you prefer.

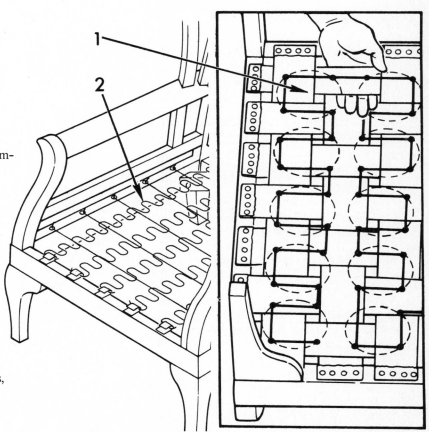

REPAIRING SAGGING SEATS

▶ Restretching Existing Webbing Bands

Restretching existing webbing consists of the following:

- Removing the tacks from one end of the bands
- Stretching the bands
- Retacking the loose ends to the rail

Restretch the front-to-back bands [1] first, then restretch the side-to-side bands [2], weaving them through the front-to-back bands.

When restretching webbing bands, always restretch the middle band first. Restretch the remaining bands by working toward the edges.

Do not remove tacks from more than one band at a time.

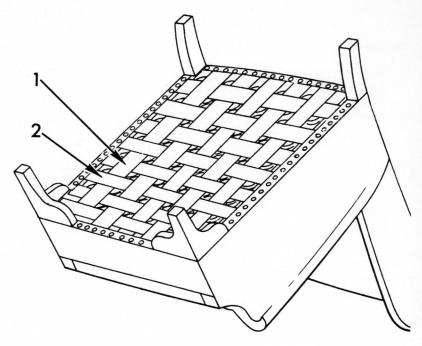

Restretching Existing Webbing Bands

Be sure to force tacks in the direction of the wood grain.

1. Using hammer and screwdriver, remove all tacks [1] from one end of band [2].

To prevent damaging the rail, use a piece of 1/8-inch or 1/4-inch wood as protection between pliers and rail.

2. Using self-locking pliers and wood block, stretch band until tight.

When driving tacks into a rail, be sure to stagger tacks. Be sure to drive tacks in the pattern and sequence [3] shown.

When driving tacks into a rail, always drive tacks as near the center of the rail as possible. Driving tacks near the rail edges may cause the rail to split.

3. Using tack hammer, drive five tacks through band into rail.

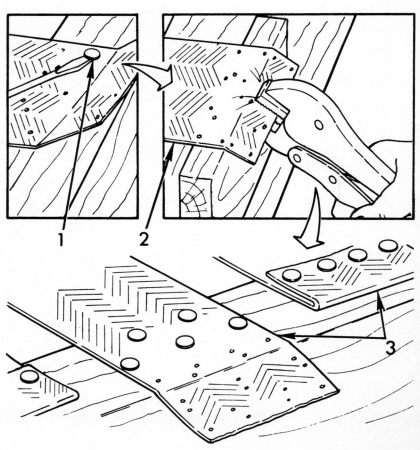

Restretching Existing Webbing Bands

4. Fold loose end of band [1] over tacks.

5. Using tack hammer, drive four tacks [2] through band into rail.

Repeat Steps 1 through 5 for all front-to-back bands.

Repeat Steps 1 through 5 for all side-to-side bands.

After all the bands are restretched, the cambrick dust cover must be installed. Go to Page 70 to install cambrick dust cover.

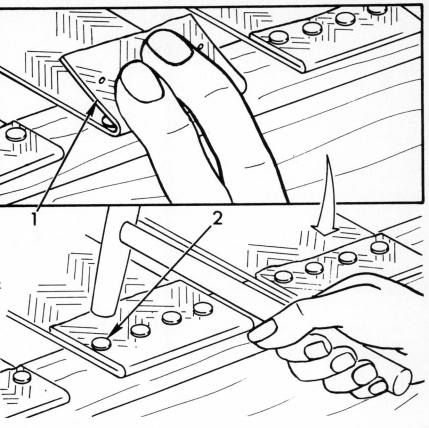

▶ Rewebbing With New Jute Webbing Bands

Rewebbing with new jute webbing bands consists of the following:

*   Cutting the twine holding the springs to the webbing bands

*   Removing the bands

*   Tying the springs at their correct height and position

*   Installing new webbing bands

1. Using scissors, cut and remove all twine [3] holding springs to webbing bands.

Be sure to force tacks in the direction of the wood grain.

2. Using hammer and screwdriver, remove all tacks [1] holding all bands [2] to frame. Remove all webbing bands.

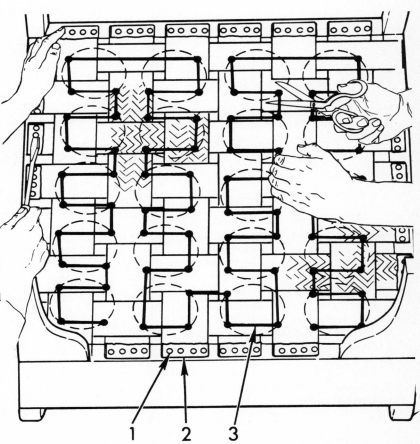

REPAIRING SAGGING SEATS

Rewebbing With New Jute Webbing Bands

The coil springs [4] must be tied at the bottom to insure their correct height and position.

The springs must be tied with their bottom coils flush with the bottom edge of the seat rails.

Tie the front-to-back rows [2] first, then tie the side-to-side rows [1].

When tying springs, always tie the middle row first. Tie the remaining rows by working toward the edges.

3. Measure distance [5] from rail to rail. Multiply distance by 2. Cut twine at distance figured.

Slip tacks are tacks [3] that are driven 1/2 their length into the frame. Slip tacks are driven at the center of the row being tied.

When driving tacks into a rail, always drive the tacks as near the center of the rail as possible. Driving tacks near the rail edges may cause the rail to split.

4. Using tack hammer, drive slip tacks [3] in opposite rails of row being tied.

Rewebbing With New Jute Webbing Bands

5. Tie one end of twine to either slip tack. Drive tack completely into rail.

When tying the springs, check the tack [1] often. If tack begins to pull from rail, drive another tack into rail with its head covering the head of the installed tack.

6. Connect all springs in row by looping twine around opposite sides [2] of each bottom coil.

The spring is at its correct height when the bottom coil is even with the bottom edge of the seat rails.

When adjusting springs to their correct height, be sure to keep them aligned in a straight row.

7. While pulling tightly on loose end of twine, push each spring to its correct height.

8. Wrap loose end of twine around slip tack [3]. Drive tack completely into rail. Cut and remove excess twine.

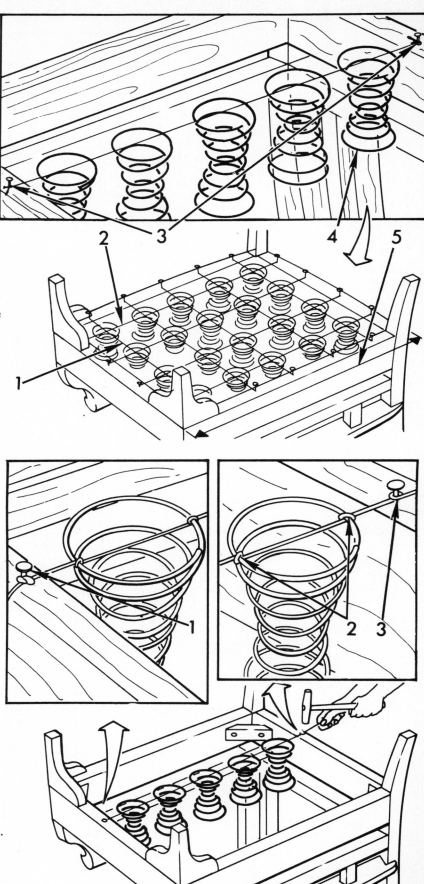

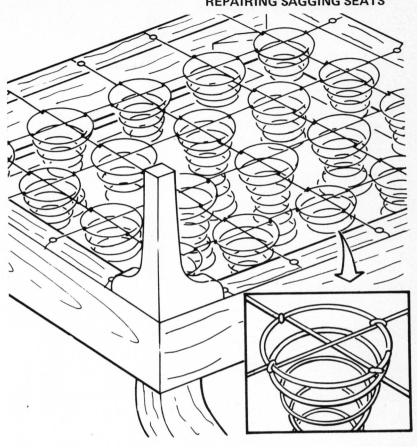

Rewebbing With New Jute Webbing Bands

Repeat Steps 5 through 8 for remaining front-to-back rows.

Repeat Steps 5 through 8 for all side-to-side rows.

After the springs are tied, the new webbing bands can be installed. Go to Page 28 to install new webbing bands.

After the new webbing bands are installed, the cambrick dust cover must be installed. Go to Page 70 to install cambrick dust cover.

▶ **Reinforcing With Steel Webbing Bands**

Reinforcing with steel webbing [1] consists of weaving and tacking the steel bands to the frame.

Stretch the front-to-back bands [5] first, then stretch the side-to-side bands [4], weaving them through the front-to-back bands.

When stretching the steel webbing bands, always stretch the middle band first. Stretch the remaining bands by working toward the edges.

If stretching perforated steel bands, a tack hole may not be located in the center of the rail. Do not drive a tack through a tack hole near the edge of the rail. Drill a hole in the band near the center of the rail and drive the tack through the drilled hole.

One steel webbing band [1] must be installed over each jute webbing band [2].

1. Place end of band [1] on rail with tack hole [3] in center of rail. Using tack hammer, drive tack through hole into rail.

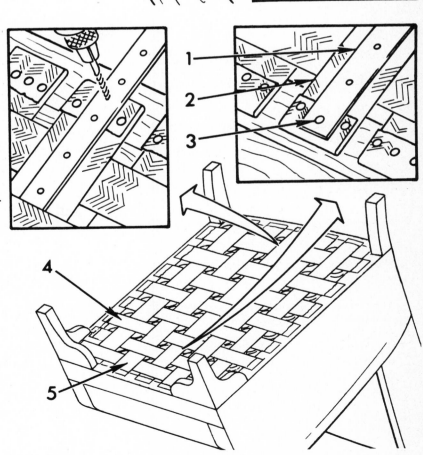

REPAIRING SAGGING SEATS

Reinforcing With Steel Webbing Bands

To prevent damaging the rail, use a piece of 1/8-inch or 1/4-inch wood [1] as protection between tool and rail.

If using steel webbing stretcher, the band [3] is stretched and tacked before cutting.

If using pliers, the band [3] is cut approximately 1 inch longer than needed. Then it is stretched and tacked. Then the excess is cut and removed.

2. Using self-locking pliers or steel webbing stretcher, stretch band [3] until springs are forced into seat and band is flat.

3. Using tack hammer, drive tack through hole [2] into center of rail.

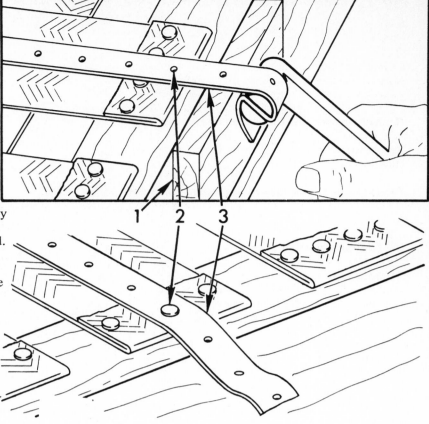

Reinforcing With Steel Webbing Bands

4. Using triangle file, file groove [1] in band near tack. Bend excess up and down until it breaks from band.

If broken end of band is bent away from the rail, it must be tacked securely to the rail with three tacks [2] to cover the sharp edges.

Repeat Steps 1 through 4 for remaining front-to-back bands.

When installing side-to-side bands, be sure to weave them through front-to-back bands.

Repeat Steps 1 through 4 for all side-to-side bands.

After all the steel webbing bands are installed, the cambrick dust cover must be installed. Go to Page 70 to install cambrick dust cover.

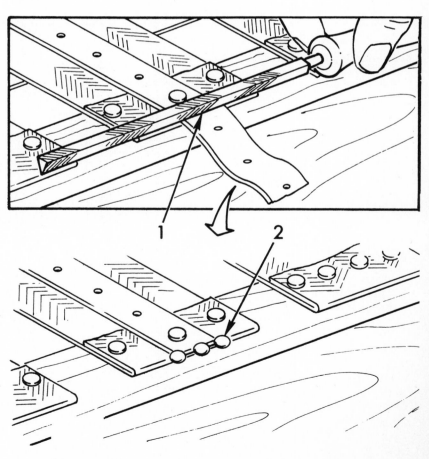

Replacements for missing buttons can be obtained from upholstery shops. Because the buttons must be covered with your upholstery material, obtain a piece of matching material to cover the button. If a matching piece is not readily available, you may be able to remove material from a hidden part of the furniture. The shop will tell you how large a piece you will need.

Procedures for replacing damaged or missing buttons or for retying loose buttons are the same.

1. Unfasten bottom [2] and side(s) [1] of back cover. Go to Page 9 for procedures for removing back cover.

2. Install or tie button(s). Go to Page 70 for procedures for installing buttons.

3. Fasten bottom and side(s) of back cover. Go to Page 67 for procedures for installing back cover.

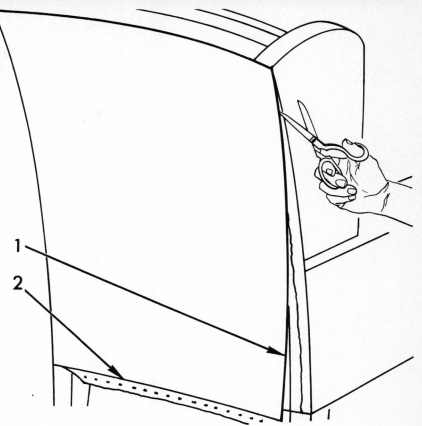

PROTECTING AND CLEANING UPHOLSTERY

The job of caring for your upholstered furniture can be greatly simplified if the fabric is coated with a fabric protector. Treated fabrics will resist staining by greasy or watery liquids. Liquids will "bead up" on the surface of the material, permitting easy clean up by blotting.

Many furniture stores offer, as a service, to treat newly purchased furniture with a fabric protector at slight additional cost. When ordering upholstered furniture, it is a good idea to specify that it be treated. It is a small investment which will help you prolong its appearance in like-new condition.

When shopping for upholstery fabrics, you will find that many fabrics have already been treated with a fabric protector by the manufacturer. Look for these materials. If you can find a treated fabric which fits your decorating scheme, you will benefit from its easier care.

If your upholstery has not been treated with a fabric protector, it is a simple job to apply it yourself. Whether you do the job or have it done by others, be sure to use a quality fabric protector.

Many of the materials used to cover upholstered furniture are designed for easy care. Only occasional cleaning is required to keep an item looking like new for years. Cleaning procedures for the more commonly used materials are as follows:

Leather. Wash with saddle soap. Saddle soap nourishes the leather and restores its pliability as well as cleaning it. Repeat applications as recommended by the manufacturer.

Plastic and Vinyl. Soil can usually be removed from these materials by washing with soap or detergent. If additional cleaning is required, apply special upholstery or vinyl cleaning products. These products are available in aerosol or paste form.

Fabric. Fabrics can be kept clean for long periods of time with occasional vacuuming. If pillows or cushions are stuffed with down, be careful when vacuuming so that down is not removed from item.

If upholstery is stained or soiled locally, try removing the spot with a spot remover. Before using a spot remover, test it on a hidden part of the fabric. Be sure that it does not damage or discolor the fabric.

Spot removers can leave a ring around the newly cleaned area. It may be possible to remove the ring or prevent the ring from appearing if spot remover is applied to a larger area around the spot. Spot-cleaning will not generally leave a ring if the fabric has been previously treated with a quality fabric protector.

If the upholstery needs an overall cleaning, apply an upholstery shampoo or cleaner. To prevent wetting the fabric, these products are used to produce a thick foam or lather. The foam or lather is then applied to the surface to remove soil. Many products are available which do an excellent job of cleaning.

After cleaning the upholstery, apply a coating of a quality fabric protector.

NOTES

NOTES

NOTES

NOTES

NOTES

NOTES

NOTES

NOTES